How to
Stay Healthy

Richard J. B. Willis

MA MSc FRSH FRIPHH AITV MIPHE

Dedicated in appreciation to

Christine Davis
Judith Willis
Laurens Willis
Gillian de Villiers
Dawn Tompkins

Copyright © 2001
The Stanborough Press Ltd.

All rights reserved.
No part of this publication may
be reproduced in any form
without permission
of the publisher.

ISBN 1-899505-74-1

First edition 2001

Published by
The Stanborough Press Ltd.,
Alma Park, Grantham,
Lincolnshire, NG31 9SL,
England.

Printed by
The Review and Herald® Publishing Association,
55 West Oak Ridge Drive,
Hagerstown, Maryland,
21740, USA.

How to Stay Healthy

Editors:
David Marshall PhD
Eileen Baildam MD

Contents

Someone Special	8
How to Stay Healthy	10
Eating for Health	14
How to Reduce Weight	17
The Benefits of Exercise	22
How to Keep in Shape	24
Reducing Heart Risks	28
Reducing Cancer Risk	32
Reducing Diabetes Risk	35
Reducing Stress	38
How to Help Your Mental Health	43
Reducing Environmental Risks	46
Reducing the Effects of Ageing	49
How to Have a Healthy Pregnancy	53
Personal Lifestyle Factors	57
How to Stop Smoking	62
Reducing Alcohol and Other Drug Risk	66
Reducing Tuberculosis Risk	71
Reducing Meningitis Risk	74
How to Help Your Eyes	77
How to Help Your Teeth and Mouth	85
How to Help Your Ears	87
Reducing Risk Using Home Treatments	89
Reducing the Risk of Sexually-Transmitted Disease	92
Postscript	95

This book is not intended as a substitute for the medical advice of physicians. Readers should consult their doctors where possible in matters relating to health and particularly in respect to symptoms that may require diagnosis or medical attention.

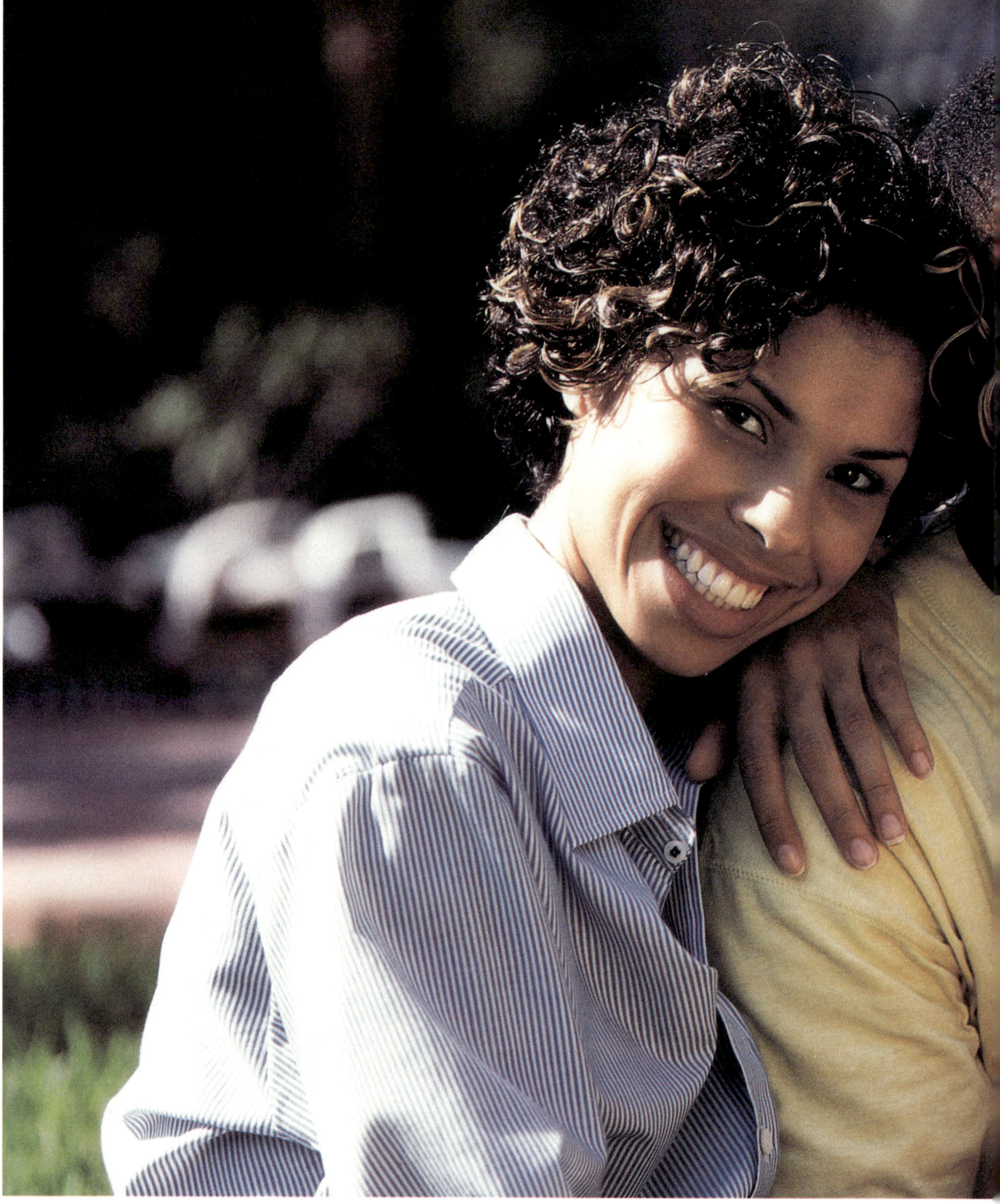

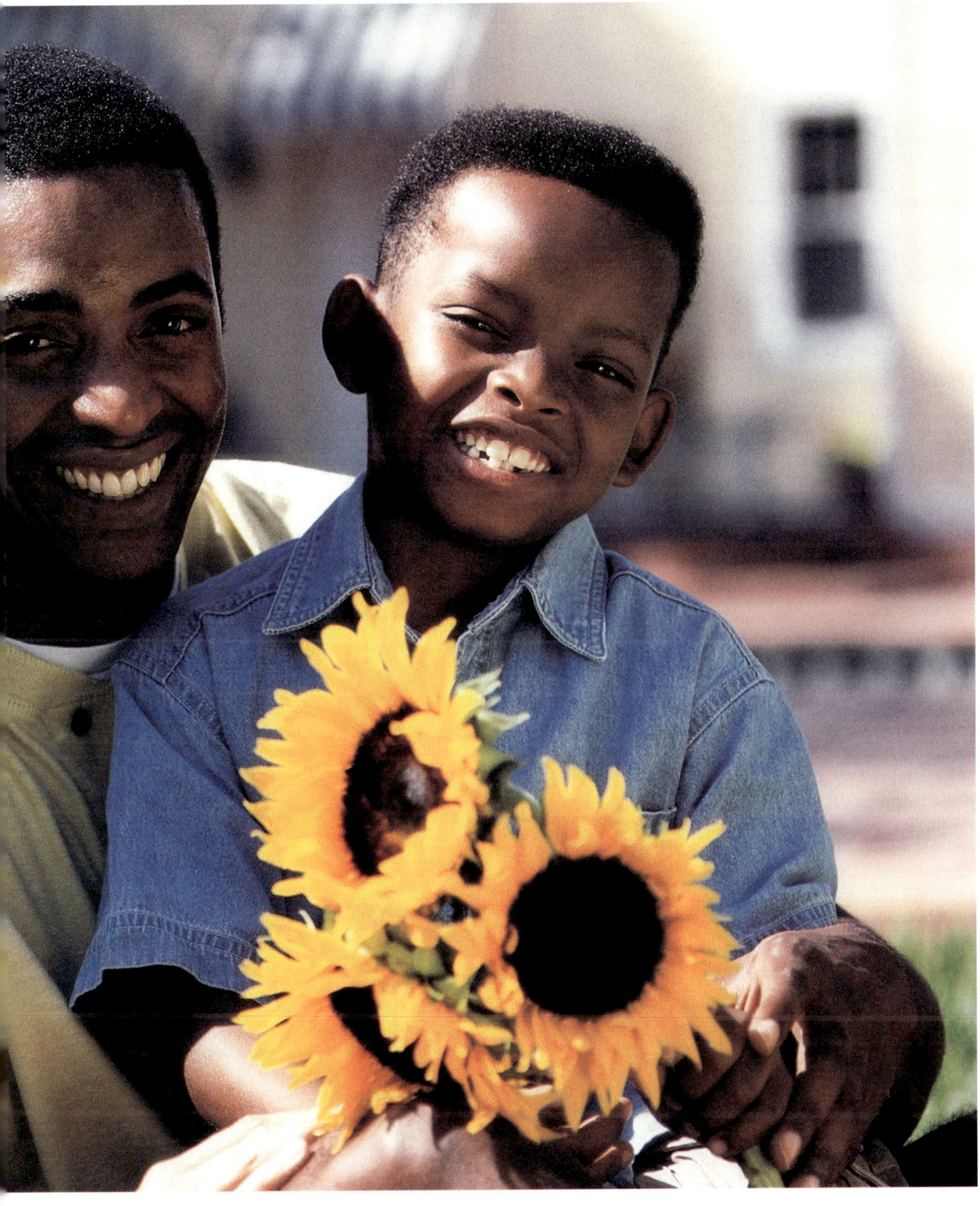

Someone Special

Unique

We sometimes stand in front of a mirror and cast a critical eye over our appearance, noting every bulge, wrinkle or sign of ageing or illness. In our more thoughtful moments we might even have wondered what is going on beneath the surface of our skin. What we see externally very often depends on what we are looking for. We may not, however, have stopped long enough to consider just how special we are individually, or to think about the complexity of our body's structure and chemistry. When we do, we discover just how unique we are.

Although we share the characteristics of others of our race and gender, no two of us – including twins – are absolutely alike. We are truly unique. In order for you to appreciate fully that uniqueness it may help to look inside the 'average' you, and take stock of some of those special features.

Body Inventory

The average 'you' weighs 147 lbs/66.6 kg and stands at 67 ins/171.45 cms. You have 206 bones and 230 joints supporting 500 separate muscles covered with 18 sq. ft/5.48 sq. metres of skin. Approximately 10 pints/4.73 litres of blood circulate around your body. At an average rate of 72 beats a minute your heart beats 103,680 times a day.

You have enough:
- **lime** for a bucketful of limewash
- **fat** for seven bars of soap
- **water** to fill a 10 gallon/45.46 litre water butt
- **iron** to make a 2 inch/5cm nail
- **carbon** to fill 9,000 lead pencils
- **phosphorus** to cover 2,200 match heads,

and you generate about 60 watts of energy – enough to heat the average household light bulb.

Your body is potentially most active at ten o'clock in the morning and seven o'clock in the evening. It is least active at one o'clock in the morning (we appear *not* to be designed for partying!)

One square centimetre of your skin contains around three million tiny cells. In that microscopic area you have:
- 1 yard/91.44 cm of blood vessels to provide nourishment
- 2 sensors to detect cold
- 4 yards/365.76 cms of nerves to carry messages
- 10 hairs
- 12 sensors to detect heat
- 15 sebaceous (oil-producing) glands to keep your skin supple
- 25 pressure organs for sensing touch
- 100 sweat glands to transport impurities
- 200 nerve endings to record pain

You have around 120,000 hairs on your scalp; more (150,000) if you are blond; fewer (90,000) if you are a redhead. These hairs grow about eighty per cent of the time and rest for the remaining twenty per cent. Body hair is slower growing (forty to fifty per cent of the day). If you are a man, your chin has 25,000 bristles which grow one hundredth of an inch (.025 cm) in twenty-four hours and probably to a lifetime maximum of 250 ins/635 cms.

Internal Activity

Even when you think you are not busy the internal work does not cease, fortunately! Every second of every day 10,000,000 red blood cells are taken out of circulation, destroyed and replaced. Your blood travels through 100,000 miles of blood vessels taking about a minute to circulate through your entire body.

If you smoke or take exercise your heart has to work harder (although for different reasons). For every 1 lb/.45 kgs of extra fat that you carry, another 200 miles/321.86 kms of blood vessels have to be made thus making your heart work even harder. In a day, you breathe 23,240 times, inhaling 20 cubic feet/1.85 cubic metres of oxygen from 7.9 quarts/1.65 litres of air, and exhaling more than 20 cubic feet of carbon dioxide; you use twice as much air when you walk (which, incidentally, is about 5 miles/8.04 kms a day or 20,000 steps which, by the time you are 80 years old is the equivalent of having walked six times around the Earth); and three times as much when you run. Naturally, from time to time you sigh – about once every three minutes – at which time you breath twice as deep as usual. Your inhaling and exhaling produces about ½lb/.227 kgs of moisture vapour an hour. Your eyes use a quarter of your body's nervous energy each day by registering somewhere in the region of 50,000 images and communicating these to your brain. A day of reading moves the eye muscles about 100,000 times. Every time you blink you shut off visual communication for three-tenths of a second, so eleven to twenty per cent of your waking time you do not see what is happening. When you sleep your eyes continue moving while you are dreaming, and you turn about 25 to 35 times in your sleep.

You speak 4,800 words as part of your general communication, more if your occupation is dependent upon it, and maybe even in your sleep.

To provide the energy for all this activity you eat 3½lbs/1.81 kgs of food. In fact, you consume your own weight in food about once every ten days if you are a healthy child, or once every fifty days as an adult. If you eat more than your body needs to provide energy, you put on weight; if less, then you lose some. Sedentary lifestyles call for a lowered energy intake. In any case, as we get older, our energy need is reduced by about five per cent for each decade of adult life.

We also lose a little height from about the age of 30 years – .0007 ins/.00017 cms – not immediately noticeable but amounting to ½in/1.27 cm over a 20-year period.

Your brain has approximately 1,000,000,000 nerve cells, each with about 1,000 interconnections. Not all of these are exercised every day. Some have specialized roles to play and others are activated according to your activity at any given moment. Their connecting network extends throughout your body and messages are sent and received by the brain at speeds between 2½ to 400 miles an hour.

Finely Tuned

There is much, much more that could be said about each part of the body and its particular, unique functions, but enough has been said to highlight the inter-relatedness of the parts described.

It should be clear that for the unique you to operate at its most efficient level you need to keep it finely tuned. We call the mode of fine tuning 'lifestyle'. The kind of lifestyle that we adopt will determine how well we function in meeting our personal and social demands. We need to stay healthy so that we can enjoy life at its fullest.

How to Stay Healthy

The Whole Person

The *World Health Organization* defines health as 'a state of total physical, mental and social well-being, not merely the absence of disease'. This definition is a recognition that we are integrated beings enjoying health in a number of inseparable dimensions each having a profound influence on the others. The *Concise Oxford Dictionary* is even more direct when it says that health is 'physical soundness, mental soundness, spiritual soundness'. We can summarize these characteristics of healthy being as lifestyle factors in which *soundness* might be alternatively described as a *quality of life*.

Lifestyle

The role of lifestyle in determining our actual health status is now seen as being of increasing importance. Current research shows that in all causes of death four factors are outstanding. Lifestyle is the leading factor, accounting for fifty-three per cent of deaths. A further twenty-one per cent are attributed to environmental factors. If we consider that we are largely able to control lifestyle and environmental factors, we can conclude that seventy-four per cent, or nearly three-quarters, of factors contributing to death lie pretty much within our ability to change for the better. Sixteen per cent of factors contributing to early death rest with our heredity. However, medical scientists tell us that even if we carry a genetic fault it is not inevitable that it will be manifested in our generation if we have minimized its appearance by adopting a healthy lifestyle. The remaining ten per cent of factors lie in the realm of health-care itself. That may seem odd on the surface but is easily explainable.

Accidents and turns for the worst occur even in hospitals. Science, even medical science, does not have all the answers to our problems. We may know what tablet A does, and even tablet B, when taken as prescribed. What we are not so sure about is what tablets A and B do when taken at the same time. Many of these insights come with more experimentation and the passing of time.

So the good news is that when we consider these factors together we see that our measure of control in all these areas is already very great and has the potential of getting better all the time.

We can only contribute to our health when we understand our bodies and their needs. This is not a new idea. The British philosopher Robert Boyle (1627-1691) said rather quaintly:

> It is highly dishonourable for a Reasonable Soul to live in so Divinely built a Mansion as the Body she resides in, altogether unacquainted with the exquisite structure of it.

He is right of course. We ought to know our bodies and how to keep them in good health, not only by ensuring that we have a positive lifestyle but also what to do when things go wrong, and there is no guarantee that they will not, as we do not live in an ideal world.

'Good' Health Habits

The current impetus for the interest in healthy living came about as a result of study into the health habits and health status of 7,000 Californians in 1972 by the researchers Lester Breslow and N. B. Belloc.

In examining the physical condition of the men and women, they concluded that people who practised a number of health habits were in better health than those who did not. In fact, seven 'good' health habits were prominent. The healthiest people in the group were people who:

✦ never smoked
✦ drank fewer than four alcoholic drinks a week [better yet, none!]
✦ took breakfast every day
✦ rarely ate between meals
✦ slept 7-8 hours nightly
✦ often engaged in exercise

- were women less than ten per cent overweight, or men less than twenty per cent overweight

Correlations could also be demonstrated between even a few of these health habits and actual health status. The research gave rise to further studies conducted elsewhere around the world and with similar results.

A Balanced Life

Another dimension of health that has become very clear is the necessity to keep a balance to our lives, not just in the integration of being in the three areas already noted but even within those areas. Put simply, we are beginning to recognize that too little input may be as harmful as excessive input. If, for example, we take health problems with possible nutritional links, we see that there is in fact an optimal diet which provides the appropriate level of resource to maintain good health.

Hypertension (or high blood pressure) may be related to a *deficiency* of potassium or calcium in the diet. On the other hand an *excess* of salt or fat might be a contributory factor. Dental cavities may be due to a *lack* of fluoride in protecting the teeth or due to the *presence* of sugars attacking the teeth. The matter of balance is brought home further when we consider the difference that vitamins, minerals, and trace elements can make to our health, even in the relatively small amounts that they represent as part of our balanced diet.

In order for disease conditions to develop, there has to be a causative agent *and* a susceptible person, although disease is not inevitable as, in spite of what is said above, there are reasonably wide margins of tolerance. However, if we adopt a positive lifestyle along the lines of the research cited, the risks can be reduced further as the individual becomes resistant. Likewise, it is not possible to guarantee absolute freedom from disease because, as has already been stated, we do not live in a perfect world.

Diseases of Affluence

Studies in war-time Europe – where food rationing was the norm – show that the general health of the population improved where the diet was restricted and fairly basic. Although we hear a lot about stress today as a cause of illness, it did not have such a major impact on health during the war when stress on an everyday basis was necessarily high.

When rationing ceased and a wider variety of foodstuff was available (either natural or processed) good health started to decline. As people ate more indiscriminately the disease statistics reflected the changes in lifestyle. Cancers and heart disease and other degenerative conditions leapt to the top of the list of causes of death and long-term ill-health. Since these changes were more often seen in Western countries with high standards of living, doctors started to describe these conditions as 'diseases of affluence'. Where there is economic growth and the adoption of the Western style of living, the diseases of affluence appear to follow. For example, breast and colon cancer rates remain low in countries where the diet is basic and the fat intake is limited. When people emigrate to the affluent countries and adopt the lifestyle of their new country, and dietary habits in particular, the breast and colon cancer rates rise to the locally observed levels. However, if the emigrants continue to follow their established dietary practices the cancer rates remain the same.

Reducing the Risks

Careful observations over a range of lifestyle factors indicate that positive changes can bring about a corresponding change in health status.

This has led governmental health departments and other non-governmental agencies dealing with health to publish recommendations which they believe will help to lower overall and particular health risks such as cancer and heart disease.

The *Europe Against Cancer* organization makes ten recommendations. First of all, they say that **'Certain cancers may be avoided'**,
+ if a person does not smoke; smokers stop as quickly as possible, and do not smoke in the presence of others,
+ if alcohol intake of beers, wines or spirits, was more moderate (preferably, none at all);
+ if individuals avoid excessive exposure to the sun, and protect themselves where this is unavoidable;
+ if workers follow health and safety instructions at work, concerning production, handling or use of any substance which may cause cancer;
+ if fresh fruits and vegetables and cereals with a high fibre content are eaten frequently;
+ if people avoid becoming overweight and also limit their intake of fatty foods;
+ if people noticing lumps, changes in 'moles' and pigmentation, or abnormal bleeding would report these to their doctor or medical centre; (Many cancers can be cured if detected early.)
+ if persistent problems such as coughs, hoarseness, changes in bladder or bowel habits, or unexplained weight loss are reported to a doctor;
+ if women have regular cervical smears;
+ if breasts are checked regularly and, where possible, mammography (a special X-ray test) is undergone at regular intervals, particularly for women above the age of fifty. Men are advised to check for testicular lumps regularly.

Specific dietary advice from various agencies shows that:
+ fruits and vegetables containing vitamin A tend to protect against epithelial (skin) tissue cancers;
+ fruits containing vitamin C inhibit the formation of nitrosamine (a carcinogen or cancer causing agent), thus helping to reduce abdominal (stomach or colon) cancers;
+ green-leafed vegetables of the cruciferous (cabbage) family help to increase colon enzymes which deactivate carcinogens, again helping to reduce colon cancers;
+ fats above twenty-four per cent of total calorie intake increase a variety of cancer risks, particularly that of breast cancer. Animal fats should be kept to a minimum in favour of vegetable fats/oils, of which the mono- and polyunsaturated fats are beneficial. The polyunsaturated fatty acids should equal one third of a person's total fat intake;
+ eating less salt-cured, salt-pickled, and smoked foods helps lower overall cancer risk.

All these dietary recommendations may be summarized in an easily remembered sentence: Eat at proper times a variety of natural foods in optimum quantities to maintain ideal weight.

Not only is this advice for would-be cancer risk reducers, it makes sound advice for people wishing to reduce the risk of heart disease. In fact, heart risk reduction agencies worldwide say that we would all benefit if we:

lowered our
+ total fat intake, and
+ reduced our intake of saturated fats (usually found in meat);

lowered our
+ calorie intake to match our ideal weight, and
+ avoided the use of refined sugars;

lowered our
+ alcohol intake where this is part of a lifestyle [alcohol is best eliminated, totally], and
+ reduced our salt intake;

increased our
+ vegetarian food intake, and in particular if we ate more complex carbohydrates (bread, pasta, legumes, cereals, and unpolished rice), and foods high in fibre such as fruits and vegetables.

Adopting these measures would help to reduce the diseases of affluence and strengthen our immune system. This would further help to protect against common seasonal infections, and the debilitating effects of newly-recognized conditions such as AIDS. So instead of being susceptible people we could exercise our potential and become resistant people with a lower incidence of a wide range of disease.

The Food We Eat

We take great pleasure in selecting and preparing food items and are attracted by food taste, texture, smell and colour. That is as it should be. We should also be choosing foods which help us to enjoy good health. We may not realize just how food can affect our health and behaviour.

Recently, there has been a new focus on that relationship. A South Bank University (London) professor of nutrition, Dr J. W. T. Dickerson, writes: 'It is now generally accepted that foods, or specific constituents of them, can make people ill.' He goes on to describe some of the clinical conditions associated with food-related illness.

Conversely, it is also fairly widely recognized that vitamins and minerals given to individuals who have a deficiency of such items can also remedy many of the physical, emotional and mental difficulties experienced. Unfortunately, many people do not have access either to good and varied food supplies, or to vitamins and minerals to help redress the problems associated with their lack. Where possible, the best ingredients should be selected and, in any case, used to the best advantage.

Our eating habits are more important than we might think, as food also plays a role in causing or relieving conditions which have social implications. Dr Dickerson highlights, for example, attention deficiency, hyperactivity, disruptive behaviour, and violent and criminal behaviour. We might be surprised by this connection. In many instances these traits were significantly reversed when 'the changes to the diets made in these trials resulted in an increase in nutrient density [more good food!] and were accomplished by replacing high fat and sugary foods, with fruits and vegetables and with whole grains'.

Fortunately, these food items form the basis of many staple diets and are enjoyed wherever they are eaten. They are the same items recommended by nutritionists promoting reduction of cancer and heart disease risk. The idea of food affecting behaviour is not new and is referred to in the writings of the Greek classics through to more recent books such as *Diet, Crime and Delinquency,* written by criminologist Alexander Schauss in 1981. In his book he quotes a pertinent statement by a famous physician from the Middle Ages, Moses Maimonides, who wrote, 'No illness which can be treated by diet should be treated by any other means.'

We are just beginning to wake up to the implications of his statement.

Professor Dickerson comments on the food/crime connection, citing a number of studies. He concludes, 'There now seems to be sufficient evidence to justify serious attention being given to a relationship between food, nutrition and truancy, expulsion from school and anti-social or violent behaviour which may result in criminality.'

These statements, coming alike from ancient philosophers, criminologists, and food scientists, challenge us to look carefully at the food we eat and understand our choices so that our deepest needs may be met, and so that we can stay healthy in every respect.

Eating for Health

As most people equate health with food – and in view of its importance who can blame them? – that is where we will start. The food that we eat should help us stay healthy by:

✦ giving us energy to go about the business of living, helping us to enjoy our work and leisure activities;

✦ building and repairing our muscles, blood, bones and teeth by providing the basic building materials;

✦ protecting our health and keeping us as free as possible from disease.

All foods meet these requirements to a greater or lesser degree. However, some foods are better than others for meeting the specific requirements of energy, building or protection. That is why we read and hear so much about balanced diets. Good nutrition includes adequate and, indeed, optimal amounts of carbohydrate, protein, fats, vitamins and minerals.

Carbohydrate

Carbohydrate provides the body with energy, and is found in two forms:

✦ **complex** (starches) which supplies the body with long-term energy as the food breaks down slowly, releasing its energy over a long period without tiring or wearing out the body.

✦ **simple** (sugars). By contrast, sugars provide a quick burst of energy that cannot be sustained, except by more food of a similar nature, causing short spurts of energy which eventually leads to tiredness and depletion of energy reserves which can be harmful to the body.

Protein

There are twenty amino acids (minute chemical building blocks) which we find in varying amounts in different types of protein. Nine of these amino acids are considered essential, so it is important that we eat foods containing them, or combinations of protein foods that help us to have an equivalent nutrient intake.

Fats

The various minute constituents of fat are vital to the chemistry of the body processes requiring only an optimal amount for that purpose. Fat is also rich in energy. An excess of fat provides an imbalance in the body chemistry and the surplus energy is stored in the body fat which can be utilized for energy if the need arises, but, unfortunately, in the meantime, contributes adversely to body weight.

All fats/oils are not the same and are described according to their chemical make-up as *monounsaturated*, *polyunsaturated*, or *saturated* fats. As far as our health is concerned, fat intake should be kept to a minimum with the mono- or polyunsaturated fats/oils being the best option.

Vitamins and Minerals

These items are also needed for vital body chemistry. Vitamins, depending on their source, are said to be either *fat soluble* (vitamins A, D and E), or *water soluble* (vitamins B and C).

The fat soluble vitamins are eaten in the fats or oils occurring naturally in plants or animal fats; used according to body need; and any excess is stored in body fat. If these stored vitamins are added to over a period of time they can become harmful to the body.

Water soluble vitamins are mostly obtained from plant sources; used in the body chemistry; and any excess, apart from some small reserve, is soluble in the body fluids and excreted in the normal way.

Minerals in very minute quantities are also needed for the physiology of the body and can be obtained from a variety of sources.

Nutritionists around the world have produced a helpful 'healthy diet pyramid' which will guide in choosing the right kind of food to provide the body requirements and are also a guide to quantity. With the exception of the inclusion of flesh foods and dairy products (where used) at the *eat-moderately level* the vegetarian right eating pyramid can be used by all to meet their nutritional needs.

The right eating pyramid
a vegetarian guide to daily food choices

Fats, oils and sweets
Eat sparingly

Beans, nuts, seeds and meat alternatives
2-4 servings
Eat moderately

Low fat or non-fat milk, yoghurt and fresh cheese
2-3 servings
Eat moderately

Fruits
2-4 servings
Eat generously

Vegetables
3-5 servings
Eat generously

Whole grains, breads, cereals, rice and pasta: 6-11 servings
Eat mostly

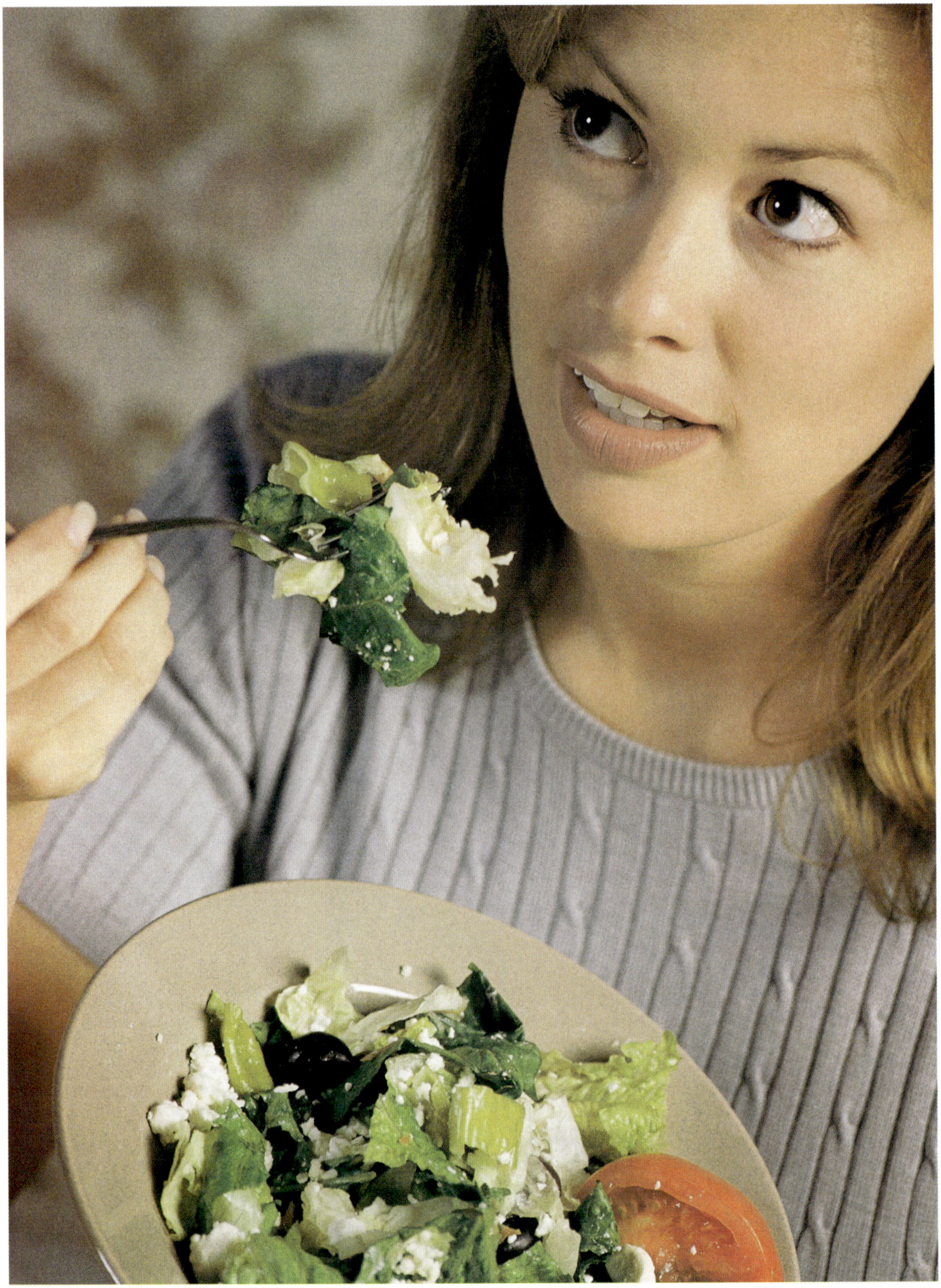

How to Reduce Weight

Using the healthy eating pyramid as a guide, and following the well-tried suggestions in this section, it should be possible to reach and maintain an ideal weight.

Eat Regularly – Three Small Meals Daily

Many people who are overweight feel that if they reduce their meals to one or two a day they will lose weight. Although there is an element of truth in the idea, even one meal a day can contain far more calories than the body needs, and the eater may not feel satisfied!

It is important, therefore, to consider the meal content and the size of the portions eaten. Ideally the first meal of the day should be larger than any subsequent meal or meals.

Breakfast is the most important meal of the day. Breakfast is literally breaking a fast. It follows the longest period of time that one is without food. That could be as long as 10-15 hours. Even while sleeping, energy is being used in the form of blood sugar to repair body tissue and to continue various physiological processes. Consequently, on waking, the body reserves of energy are at their lowest.

A good breakfast bridges the energy gap, restoring blood sugar levels and providing nutrition insurance for the rest of the day, and should contain not less than a third of the daily nutrient requirement. In any case, the body's metabolic rate (speed of digestion) is more efficient early in the day, so will deal with the food intake more appropriately.

If a third meal is taken it should be the lightest of the day. Towards evening the metabolic rate slows down for the night, so does not deal efficiently with food taken at that time.

Avoid Big Meals

This follows on naturally from what has been stated already. Someone has said, 'We should breakfast like a king, dine like a prince, and supper like a pauper.' Of course, there are always special occasions when bigger meals are taken, but these should be the exception to the rule.

It is of importance, particularly, in the case of weight control. Many a good eating habit has been spoilt by over-indulgence, especially if the weight loss has cost some effort to achieve. Some people have the mistaken idea that they should reward themselves for all their hard work in sticking to their new diet. In time, the stomach will shrink, and the attitude to eating and reward will change and ensure success in maintaining weight loss, and the cravings will disappear more easily if they are not occasionally indulged.

Get Plenty of Vitamins and Minerals

Although minute, these dietary ingredients play a big part in servicing the nervous system and in the production of hormones. It will mean choosing plenty of vegetables (especially green leaves and roots), using fresh fruits either eaten whole or in fruit salads, the fresher the better, and including citrus fruits.

Using a variety of vegetables and fruits will help to reduce craving for other foods less helpful to the body, and also reduce the craving for tobacco and/or alcohol where these are used.

Avoid Eating Between Meals

Sometimes it is inevitable that regular meal times are not observed. At such times it is easy to snack until a normal meal can be taken. The problem is that most snacks are high in calories, and do not provide the nutritional balance required since they are often high in fat, sugar, or salt.

Fresh fruit or a reasonable amount of fruit juice is a safer alternative to snacking and will carry over nutritionally to the next regular meal.

Chew Food Thoroughly

The digestive process is a long one, and gives opportunity for all kinds of medical conditions to occur along the length of the digestive tract.

Chewing food thoroughly ensures that each stage of the digestive process has the ideal conditions to function at its best.

It also has the advantage of satisfying the appetite centre in the brain and brings feelings of satiety (fullness) more quickly. In other words, eating slowly gets one tired of eating before too much is eaten.

Items to Avoid

Try to avoid too much salt and go easy on the seasoning. Salt holds on to the fluid in the tissues just as it attracts moisture in the kitchen. Research has shown that using spices, coffee, tea, sugar, cream and cigarettes increases the appetite. Additionally, caffeine and nicotine are potent insulin stimulators.

Avoid beer, wine and spirits; alcohol has a high but 'empty' calorie content. That is to say, it provides energy but has no nutritional value compared with other food items: one gram of alcohol produces 7 calories, 1 gram of fat 9 calories, 1 gram of protein produces 4.4 calories, and one gram of carbohydrate produces 4.1 calories.

As there are factors other than dietary which are involved in weight loss, the following suggestions may be useful:

✦ *Avoid Slimming Drugs*

Many people, desperate to lose weight, will try anything. These drastic measures have included stitching the mouth closed and stapling the stomach to decrease its capacity!

A considerable number of weight losers choose pills, but medicine alone is not the answer to their problem, and only a few of those people taking weight loss drugs actually need it. The few who do, have hormonal problems which make it difficult for them to shed the weight they have gained.

Some men and women may experience low function of either the pituitary or the thyroid glands. A number of women, particularly postmenopausal women, have a reduced hormone production. Screening by a physician will determine whether a hormone or metabolism test is required and the results treated appropriately.

Slimming drugs have the disadvantage of psychological and physical addiction either indirectly or directly depending on the particular drug used and the personality of the user.

✦ *Lose Weight Slowly*

There is usually short-term motivation for weight loss encouraging lose-fast techniques (the need to fit into clothes for special occasions, etc). However, it is more sensible to aim for gentle weight loss, perhaps losing at the most 3 to 5 pounds a week. Weighing should be done at the same time each day.

✦ *Take Regular Exercise*

More will be said about exercise and its advantages in the next chapter.

It is wise to start off with a moderate exercise programme and to increase gently both the range and the intensity of the exercises. Avoid keep-fit classes until you *are* fit, then go and enjoy these sessions and other leisure activities.

Remember, in order to maintain ideal weight, energy in has to be balanced by energy out. To lose weight, reduce the energy in and exceed it with energy out. It is not necessary to punish or exhaust the body with exercise. Choosing a 'user friendly' form of exercise is important since it has to be part of a long-term programme. As fitness levels increase, other activities can be added to the regime.

Body Mass Index (BMI) Scale

ft	4.8	4.9	4.10	4.11	5.0	5.1	5.2	5.3	5.4	5.5	5.6	5.7	5.8	5.9	5.10	5.11	6.0
cms	142	145	147	150	152	155	158	160	163	165	168	170	173	175	178	180	183
stn's / kgs																	
6.4 / 40	20	19	19	18	17	17	16	16	15	15	14	14	13	13	13	12	12
6.6 / 41	20	20	19	18	18	17	16	16	15	15	15	14	14	13	13	13	12
6.9 / 42	21	20	19	19	18	17	17	16	16	15	15	15	14	14	13	13	13
6.11 / 43	21	20	20	19	19	18	17	17	16	16	15	15	14	14	14	13	13
6.13 / 44	22	21	20	20	19	18	18	17	17	16	16	15	15	14	14	14	13
7.1 / 45	22	21	21	20	19	19	18	18	17	17	16	16	15	15	14	14	13
7.3 / 46	23	22	21	20	20	19	18	18	17	17	16	16	15	15	15	14	14
7.6 / 47	23	22	22	21	20	20	19	18	18	17	17	16	16	15	15	15	14
7.8 / 48	24	23	22	21	21	20	19	19	18	18	17	17	16	16	15	15	14
7.10 / 49	24	23	23	22	21	20	20	19	18	18	17	17	16	16	15	15	15
7.12 / 50	25	24	23	22	22	21	20	20	19	18	18	17	17	16	16	15	15
8 / 51	25	24	24	23	22	21	20	20	19	19	18	18	17	17	16	16	15
8.3 / 52	26	25	24	23	23	22	21	20	20	19	18	18	17	17	16	16	16
8.5 / 53	26	25	25	24	23	22	21	21	20	19	19	18	18	17	17	16	16
8.7 / 54	27	26	25	24	23	22	22	21	20	20	19	19	18	18	17	17	16
8.9 / 55	27	26	25	24	24	23	22	21	21	20	19	19	18	18	17	17	16
8.11 / 56	28	27	26	25	24	23	22	22	21	21	20	19	19	18	18	17	17
9 / 57	28	27	26	25	25	24	23	22	21	21	20	20	19	19	18	18	17
9.2 / 58	29	28	27	26	25	24	23	23	22	21	21	20	19	19	18	18	17
9.4 / 59	29	28	27	26	26	25	24	23	22	22	21	20	20	19	19	18	18
9.6 / 60	30	29	28	27	26	25	24	23	23	22	21	21	20	20	19	19	18
9.9 / 61	30	29	28	27	26	25	24	24	23	22	22	21	20	20	19	19	18
9.11 / 62	31	29	29	28	27	26	25	24	23	23	22	21	21	20	20	19	19
9.13 / 63	31	30	29	28	27	26	25	25	24	23	22	22	21	21	20	19	19
10.1 / 64	32	30	30	28	28	27	26	25	24	24	23	22	21	21	20	20	19
10.3 / 65	32	31	30	29	28	27	26	25	24	24	23	22	22	21	21	20	19
10.6 / 66	33	31	31	29	29	27	26	26	25	24	23	23	22	22	21	20	20
10.8 / 67	33	32	31	30	29	28	27	26	25	25	24	23	22	22	21	21	20
10.10 / 68	34	32	31	30	29	28	27	27	26	25	24	24	23	22	21	21	20
10.12 / 69	34	33	32	31	30	29	28	27	26	25	24	24	23	23	22	21	21
11 / 70	35	33	32	31	30	29	28	27	26	26	25	24	23	23	22	22	21
11.3 / 71	35	34	33	32	31	30	28	28	27	26	25	25	24	23	22	22	21
11.5 / 72	36	34	33	32	31	30	29	28	27	26	26	25	24	24	23	22	21
11.7 / 73	36	35	34	32	32	30	29	29	27	27	26	25	24	24	23	23	22
11.9 / 74	37	35	34	33	32	31	30	29	28	27	26	26	25	24	23	23	22
11.11 / 75	37	36	35	33	32	31	30	29	28	28	27	26	25	24	24	23	22
12 / 76	38	36	35	34	33	32	30	29	28	27	27	26	25	25	24	23	23
12.2 / 77	38	37	36	34	33	32	31	30	29	28	27	27	26	25	24	24	23
12.4 / 78	39	37	36	35	34	32	31	30	29	29	28	27	26	25	25	24	23
12.6 / 79	39	38	37	35	34	33	32	31	30	29	28	27	26	26	25	24	24
12.8 / 80	40	38	37	36	35	33	32	31	30	29	28	28	27	26	25	25	24
12.11 / 81	40	39	37	36	35	34	32	32	30	30	29	28	27	26	26	25	24
12.13 / 82	41	39	38	36	35	34	33	32	31	30	29	28	27	27	26	25	24
13.1 / 83	41	39	38	37	36	35	33	32	31	30	29	29	28	27	26	26	25
13.3 / 84	42	40	39	37	36	35	34	33	32	31	30	29	28	27	27	26	25
13.5 / 85	42	40	39	38	37	35	34	33	32	31	30	29	28	28	27	26	25
13.8 / 86	43	41	40	38	37	36	34	34	32	32	30	30	29	28	27	27	26
13.10 / 87	43	41	40	39	38	36	35	34	33	32	31	30	29	28	27	27	26
13.12 / 88	44	42	41	39	38	37	35	34	33	32	31	30	29	29	28	27	26
14 / 89	44	42	41	40	39	37	36	35	33	33	32	31	30	29	28	27	27
14.2 / 90	45	43	42	40	39	37	36	35	34	33	32	31	30	29	28	28	27
cms	142	145	147	150	152	155	158	160	163	165	168	170	173	175	178	180	183
ft	4.8	4.9	4.10	4.11	5.0	5.1	5.2	5.3	5.4	5.5	5.6	5.7	5.8	5.9	5.10	5.11	6.0

Healthy Range: 19-24   Overweight: 25-29   Obese: 30+

How to Reduce Weight 21

The Benefits of Exercise

Mark Twain, the writer of *The Adventures of Huckleberry Finn*, said that if he ever thought about taking exercise he would rest until the feeling went away! As long ago as 1873 Edward Stanley, Earl of Derby, commented: 'Those who think that they have no time for bodily exercise will sooner or later have to find time for illness.'

Feeling Fit

If we want to minimize the risk of illness exercise plays a major role. Fitness involves three related factors:

- cardiopulmonary fitness;
- muscular flexibility;
- muscular strength.

A heart disease study conducted on men and women in California looked at the percentage of men dead at the end of a nine-year period. In particular the investigators wanted to establish the role of exercise in protecting against heart disease. The men and women were divided into three groups: those who exercised frequently, sometimes, or never. The first two groups were further subdivided in qualitative terms as vigorous or moderate exercisers. Research showed that of the frequent exercisers 6.8 per cent of the vigorous and 11.8 per cent of the moderate exercisers had died. Of the group who sometimes exercised 12.4 per cent who exercised vigorously and 15 per cent of the moderate exercisers had died. The highest death rate, 18.6 per cent, was in the non-exercising group. Clearly the time and quality of exercise had played a significant role. The results for the women in the study showed a similar pattern: 6.5 per cent for both the vigorous and moderate exercisers in the frequent category; 7.6 and 8.2 per cent for those who exercised moderately; and 16.1 per cent for the never exercisers. The exercisers in these and other studies felt fit – mentally and physically and scored better on tests recording psychological values.

Strength and flexibility of muscles come with practice and allow the exerciser to extend his or her repertoire of activities without getting too breathless.

The Benefits of Exercise

The benefits of exercise are numerous. We have seen how it reduces heart disease. It does this by strengthening the heart muscles, thus providing a slower but more efficient beat so that the blood circulation is also improved. Breathing is improved too, and the body benefits from the better oxygen intake and use.

Exercise builds a good body and beautifies the complexion; gives a better self concept and builds good muscles and bones (decreasing the likelihood of osteoporosis later on in life); increases resistance to disease by strengthening the immune system; reduces stress; strengthens the mind – in fact the brain requires one fifth of all the oxygen taken into the body – reduces fatigue and relaxes the nerves; and, not least, aids digestion and appetite.

Keeping Fit

You have to be fit in order to keep fit. So exercise should gently increase until you can exercise at a high level. If you are already beginning to show signs of ageing or have a health problem it is wise to get the approval of your healthcare provider. Generally speaking, walking will help most conditions if you are not able to do anything more strenuous. Walk a set distance comfortably and time yourself. Try to improve on the time in subsequent walks, feeling comfortable at each level. Then extend the distance until you have a quite vigorous walking exercise programme. You do not have to punish yourself to be fit. The 'no pain-no gain' concept is a myth. It is important to make sure that you are fit *before* adding leisure activities to your programme. You will then enjoy these activities more. Occasionally indulging in strenuous recreational pursuits may do more harm than good if you are not at a reasonable level of fitness.

For good heart health, once you are fit, you will need to exercise with greater intensity. You can calculate your exercise pulse rate by subtracting your age from 180. This gives you a target rate between 75 and 80 per cent of your maximum heart rate. Take your pulse at the wrist to see when you have arrived at this peak. You will need some warm-up and wind-down exercises and will need to keep your heart rate at the target level for about 20 minutes. Exercises at this level need only be done every other day.

Exercise for Life

It is not everyone who has the opportunity for outside or gymnastic work. Still, you can incorporate exercise into your daily work and home routine, bending and stretching muscles appropriately through the day. However, as only about 2 per cent of the population get enough exercise through their work, a home exercise machine of some kind may be of benefit. Motivation is important as without it much of what you do will seem to be boringly repetitious. Variety of approach will help to keep the motivation alive.

You can incorporate all sorts of reasons for doing your exercise to strengthen your motivation: such as decreasing your risk of heart disease; or osteoporosis; exercise is the single most effective intervention in normalizing non-insulin dependent diabetes; or whatever you think will help your resolve.

Try to include other family members in your exercise plans but remember that you are not all at the same level of fitness. If you have gymnasium or swimming facilities you can share exercise times; but attempt different circuits or lengths to suit the individual. Naturally, once you are all reasonably fit you can synchronize your efforts by taking part in the same recreational activity.

Suit Yourself

Not only is it best to engage in activities that you enjoy, it is also important to dress for the occasion. While it is not necessary to go in for designer clothes, shoes, or equipment, using the appropriate attire will help to minimize any personal discomfort or risks.

There are so many activities to choose from that the opportunities are limitless. Suit yourself and be motivated, literally, to exercise for life. It surely beats finding time for illness!

How to Keep in Shape

The following exercises can be used as a workout for 30 minutes, 3 times a week. For maximum benefit, stretches should be held for 20-30 seconds at the point of comfortable tension. Remember always to work both sides of the body. Always drink plenty of water before, during and after exercise to remain hydrated.

1. Neck and Shoulder Stretch

Stand relaxed and hold the wrist behind the back. Gently pull the shoulder down and across and tip the head away.

2. Chest, Spine and Shoulder Stretch

Kneel and align the hips over the knees. Slide the hands forward but do not allow the hips to move forward. Allow the chest to drop towards the floor.

3. Triceps Stretch

Lift the elbow above the head and drop forearm behind the head. Slide forearm down the middle of the back. Support the elbow with opposite hand and apply gentle pressure (avoid leaning to one side).

4. Lateral Raise to Strengthen Shoulders (Deltoids)

Start with hands by the sides, slowly raise to shoulder height and lower (with or without hand weights).

5. Upper Back and Shoulder Stretch

Stand relaxed with soft knees. Leaning forward, grasp the back of the thighs. Pull away from the legs leading with upper back. Allow the shoulder blades to slide apart and keep the head in a neutral position.

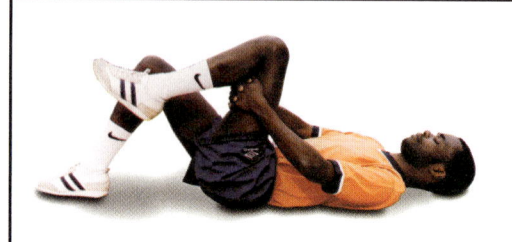

6. Spine Stretch

Lay supine (face up) with bent knees. Gently bring one knee towards the chest and hold. Bring second knee to the chest and hold.

7. Trunk Stretch

Lay prone (face down) with elbows tucked into the side of the body and the hands under the shoulders. Gently lift the upper body, pressing the chest up and forward (avoid lifting elbows from floor).

8. Groin Stretch

Support the body on all fours and slowly extend one leg to the side. Press the groin towards the floor while leaning backwards slightly.

9. Kneeling Hip Flexor Stretch

Kneeling, take one foot forward as far as comfort allows. Gently lean forward pressing the groin forwards and towards the floor. Align the front knee directly over the ankle or shoelace, (avoid knee protruding beyond the shoelace).

10. Standing Hip Flexor and Quadricep Stretch

Stand, using a wall or partner for balance and support. Lift one foot behind, holding the ankle with corresponding hand. Soften the other knee and gently press the hips forward (avoid bent knee moving sideways away from the body).

11. Hamstring Stretch

Keep back straight and one knee bent to support body weight. Sit back into the stretch, lifting tail bone up and out.

12. Lying Quadricep Stretch

Lying on the side, support the body by resting the head on the hand or upper arm. Bottom leg is forward and slightly bent to assist in balance. Bend the top leg and take the foot behind, holding the ankle with corresponding hand. Press hips forward, keeping the knees parallel to the floor.

Reducing Heart Risks

We are all conscious of the risk of heart disease. Family members, work colleagues and friends get heart disease and many die of it. Tragically, the age at which people are affected and die seems to be lower with the passage of time. Our frenetic lifestyle is at a price.

It is tempting to believe that we would receive fair warning of personal heart disease, but that is not generally the case. Although heart disease can be present in the body from an early age, we are often only aware of its presence when it is too late or almost too late to do something about it. Apart from the general need to be alert to the possibility of heart disease we need to be especially careful if other close family members have a history of the condition.

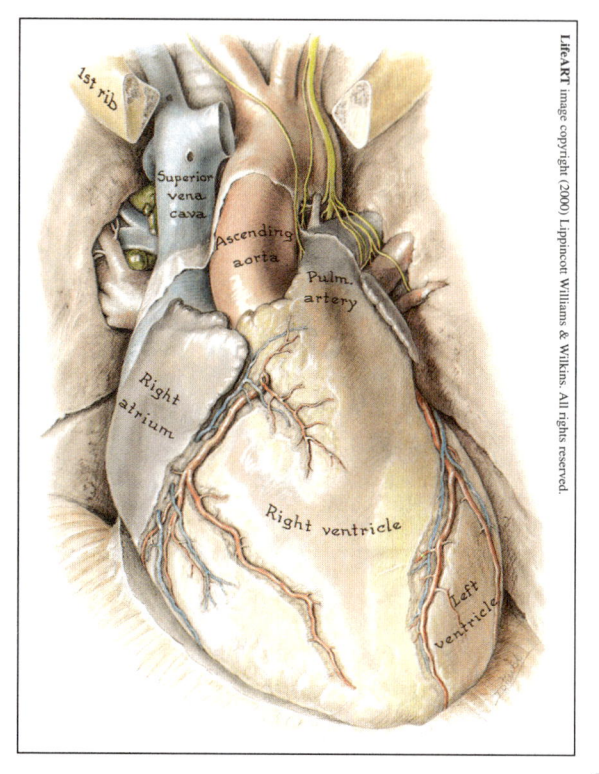

Risk Factors

Clinicians have divided the risk factors for heart disease, according to their relative value, into **primary** and **secondary** risks. Although there is some difference of opinion as to what should appear in which list overall the following risks are agreed:

Primary risk factors
- obesity;
- cigarette smoking;
- hypertension (high blood pressure);
- high blood cholesterol.

Secondary risk factors
- physical inactivity;
- low levels of protective HDL (high density lipoprotein) cholesterol;
- diabetes;
- stress;
- excessive alcohol intake;
- the oestrogen content of some contraceptive pills.

Other factors such as family history of heart disease, personality and hardness or softness of water all play a part.

Generally speaking,
- the more cigarettes smoked the greater the risk;
- the higher the blood cholesterol and the less exercise taken, the greater the risk;
- if parents are long-lived there is decreased risk for their children;
- people who are overweight and/or have diabetes are at increased risk;
- individuals with stress and/or aggressive personalities are at greater risk; there is greater risk where soft drinking water is used.

These risk factors are accumulative as well as being inherently risky.

Reducing Heart Risks

- Just using cigarettes increases your heart risk one and a half times;
- if you use cigarettes and you have a high blood cholesterol you have a three times greater risk;
- and, if you add high blood pressure to your list of woes your risk is five times more likely.

It is not only your heart that is put at the risk of disease. There are other problems associated with your circulatory system:

- If you have high blood pressure your risk of stroke is three times greater;
- if you are generally physically inactive you are twice more likely to have a stroke;
- if you do not exercise, but do smoke *and* have high blood pressure you are *twelve times more likely* to have a stroke because *these risk factors multiply*.

The Cholesterol Factor

We read and hear a lot about cholesterol and its role in heart disease. It is the stuff that adheres to the internal walls of arteries, gradually blocking them and reducing the flow of oxygen to important organs such as the brain and the heart with its resultant damage and, in many cases, contributing to the death of the individual.

The average cholesterol in a 140 lb/63.5 kg person is around 4.93 oz/140 gms; and in the blood is about 150 – 250 milligrams per 100 millilitres.

Your liver produces cholesterol, which it uses as part of the chemistry of hormone production and the bile acids used in digestion. Dietary saturated fat is converted in the liver to cholesterol and it is also absorbed directly from some of the food that we eat – such as eggs – although our body has no need of external cholesterol. Other dietary and genetic factors along with obesity influence the amount absorbed.

The cholesterol that comes from outside the body is different from that which is manufactured in the body. Dietary cholesterol is called low density lipoprotein (LDL), and it promotes the deposition of fatty substances in the artery wall. Over time this deposit accumulates and so high levels of LDL are associated with high rates of heart disease. Cholesterol produced in the body is a protective cholesterol and is called high density lipoprotein (HDL). HDL removes the fatty deposits of LDL from the artery wall and recycles it to HDL. High levels of HDL are associated with low levels of heart disease. Our bodies produce less HDL if they are receiving dietary cholesterol. The ratio of HDL to LDL is therefore an important indicator of heart risk. A blood test will determine the total cholesterol present – as well as this critical ratio – and the presence of other blood chemistry increasing the risk of heart disease.

relaxation technique and eliminate, as far as possible, the causes of their stress.

Along with these sensible measures there are also sound dietary recommendations for the reduction of harmful cholesterol.

We need to reduce:
- total fat intake and keep the saturated fat part of that to a minimum;
- calories to match our ideal weight;
- refined sugars which will quickly and easily push the calories up;
- alcohol intake – if used at all – since alcohol weakens heart muscle as well as providing unnecessary calories;
- salt intake – raised quantities of which are associated with high blood pressure.

We need to increase:
- vegetarian-type foods;
- complex carbohydrates – brown rice, wholemeal pasta and breads – with their high fibre content;
- use of grains, vegetables and fruits.

For added enjoyment, a wide variety of legumes, fruits, vegetables and grains should be used where possible. Taste will return and the heart will benefit from all these special measures.

Remedying the Risk

We cannot do too much about heredity, advancing age, and some environmental factors, but we can minimize the risk by adopting a healthy lifestyle and avoiding any extra, unnecessary risks.

Clearly, the implications of many of these risks suggest their own remedy:

- The obese need to lose weight;
- smokers need to quit smoking;
- the inactive need to exercise. A regular walking programme – whether short, intermediate, or long – reduces harmful cholesterol levels and raises the protective ones. A short walk need be only 5-10 minutes twice a day, or a long walk taking 20-40 minutes. Anything better than these can be considered a healthful bonus;
- the stressed need to learn and practise a regular

Reducing Heart Risks 31

Reducing Cancer Risk

A *Europe Against Cancer* leaflet produced as part of a cancer reduction programme asks the question *'Is cancer on your agenda?'* While many people fear the onset of any form of cancer, relatively few have taken the necessary steps to reduce the possibility. From an early age cancer needs to be on our personal agenda. After heart disease it is the next most important cause of death worldwide.

Cancer is started when the cell DNA is damaged following exposure to a carcinogen (cancer-causing agent). The cell multiplies at an uncontrolled rate, resulting in the abnormal cells forming a tumour. The tumourous growth may affect adjoining tissues and spread to other parts of the body, leading to secondary tumours.

In spite of its fearsome reputation as a killer the good news is that it can be avoided in some of its forms and markedly reduced in incidence in others. One of the world's leading cancer researchers, Professor Sir Richard Doll, says:

> On a worldwide scale the differences in incidence that have been observed encourage the belief that all the common types of cancer are largely avoidable, in the sense that it should be possible to reduce the risk of developing each type by at least a half and often by 80 per cent or more.

Ernst Wynder, former president of the American Health Foundation, states:

> It is our current estimate that some 50% of all female cancers in the western world and about one-third of all male cancers are related to nutritional factors.

While it is true that not all cancers are caused by diet, our diet either exacerbates the problems or protects us against them.

It has been estimated that about one-third of all cancers are directly related to diet and alcohol; one-third to tobacco use; and the remaining one-third due to all other factors. This latter third would include occupational hazards, pollution, industrial products, infections, some medicines and medical procedures, and other as yet unknown causes. The top three causes of cancer death in men are lung cancer, colon cancer, and cancer of the prostate. In women the three leading causes of cancer deaths are breast cancer, colon cancer, and cancers of the ovaries and uterus.

The Regional Cancer Context

A higher than average incidence of some forms of cancer is to be found on the continent of Africa. This includes:

Cancer of the Liver

✦ This is the commonest cancer in males, with the

highest rate in the world occurring in Shangaan-Tsonga men living in Mozambique;

✦ Usually associated with liver infections, high alcohol intake (and following *cirrhosis* of the liver), or spread from cancers anywhere else in the body;

✦ Characterized by pain in the upper right abdomen, *jaundice* and a fluid distension of the abdomen *(ascites).*

Treatment

✦ Difficult to treat even if detected early;

✦ Diagnosis confirmed by ultrasound scanning and liver biopsy;

✦ Removal of the tumour may be possible, otherwise the progress of the condition may be slowed by anti-cancer drugs;

✦ Abstaining from alcohol (while the damage has already been done, to continue drinking will only hasten death);

✦ In some circumstances a liver transplant might be considered.

Cancer of the Oesophagus (gullet)

✦ Particularly common in Xhosa men in South Africa (second only to north-east Iran);

✦ Difficulty in swallowing at first, and eventually reaching a painful state when it may be too late to treat successfully;

✦ Mainly related to drinking very hot fluids, smoking and alcohol.

Treatment

✦ Barium swallow and X-ray to confirm diagnosis, with a tissue biopsy if necessary;

✦ Radiotherapy and chemotherapy;

✦ Avoidance of hot fluids, smoking and alcohol.

Cancer of the Cervix (neck of the womb)

✦ Commonest cancer in black women.

✦ May be caused by erosion of the tissue cells, infections, a polyp (growth), a tear (following childbirth), or a wart resulting from a virus (*human papillomavirus* HPV) of which there are a number of high-risk strains. PHV16 and HPV18 have been present in around 90 per cent of squamous-type cancers of the cervix, and also in 50-70 per cent of pre-cancerous conditions;

✦ Having early sex and many sexual partners increases the risk of cervical cancer;

✦ Cigarette smoking may be a contributory factor;

✦ The more pregnancies, the greater the risk;

✦ Use of oral contraceptive pills may increase the risk slightly;

✦ There may be a genetic factor not yet identified;

✦ If untreated the cancer will spread to other pelvic organs.

Treatment

✦ Changes in the tissue of the cervix may be detected by smear tests *(PAP smear)* which may be followed by colposcopy (use of instrument called a colposcope for investigating cervix and womb), and biopsy if a cancer is suspected;

✦ electrocoagulation, diathermy, radiotherapy and/or chemotherapy depending on extent of the condition;

- Surgical removal of the cervix and any other affected organs;
- Early detection and treatment offers the best survival rate.

General Cancer Sites

The top three cancers listed earlier as causing male and female deaths are to be found everywhere but with varying degrees of incidence. The latest available annual World Health Organization figures show:

- Deaths worldwide from all malignant neoplasms (new growths) amount to 1,174,112 for men, and 968,351 for women;
- Colon cancer kills 62,039 men, and 70,080 women;
- Breast cancer kills 134,081 women, and 5 men;
- 33,716 ovarian cancer, and 10,477 cancer of the uterus deaths;
- 95,505 men died of prostate cancer;
- Cancers of the trachea, bronchus and lung killed 365,549 men and 132,104 women.

Not every country reports, so these figures are only as accurate as the reporting. Therefore they are likely to be under-reported. Consider also the number of people who have either been treated or who are currently undergoing treatment and you will gain a more complete picture of how cancer can cause such massive problems worldwide.

Now seems like a good time to put 'cancer on our agenda'. If we do, we can be encouraged by knowing that our risk of any of these conditions can be markedly reduced, and that early detection increases our recovery chances. Risk can be reduced further by avoiding, where possible, exposure to things known to cause cancer.

Reducing Diabetes Risk

Diabetes is one of the oldest conditions associated with nutrition and has been reported in medical literature over at least a two-thousand-year period. 'Diabetes', said the Greek writer Aretaeus (AD30-90), 'is . . . a melting down of the flesh and limbs into urine . . . . The patient never stops making water. The flow is incessant as if from the opening of aqueducts . . . . Thirst is unquenchable . . . . One cannot stop them either from drinking or making water. If for a time they abstain from drinking, their mouths become parched and their bodies dry . . . and at no distant term they expire.'! Fortunately, while the symptoms of diabetes remain much the same, the outlook is no longer bleak.

We do not know how many diabetic patients Aretaeus had but we do know that there are now 120 million diabetics worldwide. The World Health Organization estimates that this figure will escalate at the rate of one new diabetic every 40 seconds to reach a worldwide total of 300 million by the year 2025. The highest risk of diabetes is now to be found in developing countries.

Glucose Balance

During the process of digestion foods are broken down into their constituent parts and absorbed via the bowel into the bloodstream for use and for storage against future need. *Glucose* is one of these items. Glucose for the normal metabolism circulates in the bloodstream and any glucose in excess of requirement is transported to the liver and stored as *glucogen*.

A regulatory substance called *insulin*, produced by the 'islets of Langerhans' in the pancreas, controls the availability of glucose in the blood to be used for energy and how much is to be kept in reserve as glycogen.

For most people the balance between insulin production and available glucose is not a problem. Problems arise when the pancreas is not able to produce insulin or if its mechanism is impaired in some way, perhaps as a result of an inherent fault, damage or viral infection. Without the presence of insulin to regulate it, the body sugar rises to such a level that it cannot be reabsorbed back into the blood, so it is passed out of the body in the urine, much as old Aretaeus describes. Continuous and sudden draining of the body's glucose throws the whole system into shock and, because fat is metabolized, the body may build up toxic levels of *ketones* (a condition known as ketosis) which may lead to diabetic coma.

Diabetes has become associated with sugar intake in popular thinking. This is probably because the condition used to be known as 'sugar' diabetes. However, it was the 'sugar' released in the urine that gave it its name and not the sugar taken in the diet. That is not to say that sugars do not have a role to play, but current research implicates fat metabolism as the deciding factor – the higher the fat intake (particularly of saturated fats), the greater the risk of diabetes.

Types of Diabetes

There are two types of diabetes called simply *Type I* and *Type II*:

Type I
- is referred to as *Insulin Dependent Diabetes* (IDD);
- it affects 28 million people worldwide;
- caused by a malfunction of the pancreatic islets;
- used to be called *juvenile onset diabetes* since it occurs mainly in children and young adults;
- is of sudden onset;
- can be hereditary; 1:100 risk if one parent is diabetic, the risk rising if both parents are affected;
- as its name (IDD) implies, insulin is required to restore the balance.

Type II
- referred to as *Non-Insulin Dependent Diabetes* (NIDD);
- it affects 92 million people worldwide, and in developing countries is the almost exclusive form of diabetes;

- formerly called *maturity onset diabetes* since it generally occurs in the 'mature' years, affecting 1:25 persons over 65 years of age;
- it often runs in families;
- insufficient insulin produced by the pancreas;
- may be adjusted with diet and exercise; drugs may also be used where necessary.

Some ethnic groups are more susceptible to developing diabetes than others. Afro-Caribbeans are twice as likely as the general population to have diabetes, of which 4.5 per cent will be of Type I. Of the 95 per cent of Afro-Caribbeans with Type II, 30 per cent can be treated with tablets; 50 per cent treated with tablets and diet; and 20 per cent by a modified diet alone. All should be encouraged to develop and sustain a healthy lifestyle. The exercise aspect of the programme is particularly important and may make all the difference in insulin/glucose balance in the non-insulin dependent diabetic. In any case, each diabetic will be advised to keep an eye on his or her weight.

Symptoms of Diabetes

Along with the symptoms described by Aretaeus we can add: tiredness; itching around the genital area; and blurred vision. This latter symptom, if noticed early and dealt with quickly, may save running the risk of severe eye problems later. Diabetes is a leading cause of blindness, especially in persons between the ages of 20 and 74. Blindness from Type II diabetes includes cataracts (the longer diabetes is present, the higher the likelihood of cataracts), retinopathy (in which the retina or 'screen' of the eye is progressively destroyed), glaucoma (in which the pressure in the eye increases and destroys the visual nerves), and diseases of the cornea.

Cataract

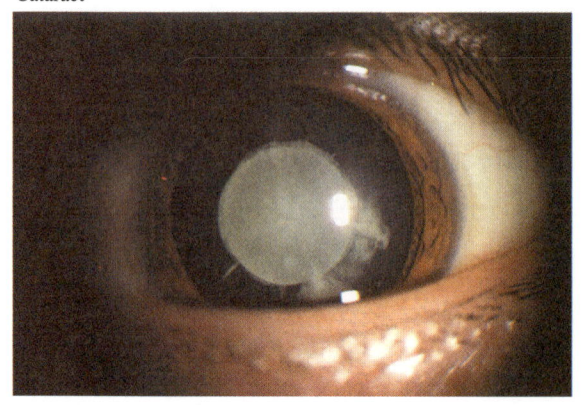

In addition to eye problems, untreated diabetes contributes to coronary artery disease; peripheral vascular diseases and stroke; impotence; is a common cause of renal (kidney) failure; and amputation.

Dietary Considerations

The following dietary recommendations will help to reduce the incidence and severity of diabetes. Although there are special foods prepared commercially for diabetics there is no necessity for their use:
- eat regular meals based on complex carbohydrates (starchy foods: whole-grain products, brown rice, wholemeal pastas, etc);
- eat high-fibre foods;
- reduce the intake of fried and fatty foods (butter, margarine, cooking oils, fatty meats and cheese). Fat intake reduced to 10-15 per cent of total calorie intake has often brought the diabetic back into range within two months. Do not severely reduce your fat intake or you will be deficient in the fat-soluble vitamins (A, D, E), and also raise your blood cholesterol;
- reduce the intake of visible and invisible sugars;
- keep to an ideal weight;
- avoid the use of salt;
- avoid alcohol (if used);
- follow any specific advice given by your healthcare professional.

Total Lifestyle

Once again we see that a natural diet along with an exercise programme helps to reduce the risk of disease. Eat fruit as fresh as possible and just under-ripe rather than over-ripe where the sugar content is more concentrated. Eating the fruit in as natural a state as possible will also provide fibre.

In spite of Aretaeus's graphic portrayal of diabetes it is a condition that can often be remedied by taking simple lifestyle measures. What is necessary to keep insulin and glucose in balance is ideal for keeping life in balance generally.

Reducing Diabetes Risk 37

Reducing Stress

Most of us seem to manage the everyday things of life without too much difficulty but when something extraordinary comes along we deal with it quite differently, with some people able to cope well and others just going to pieces. Few of us grow up learning the business of life directly. We observe how our parents, family and other leaders deal with problems and file the information away in our minds until a similar situation confronts us personally. Sometimes what we have learnt suits the circumstances, at other times we are at a loss as to what to do.

Distress

We cannot avoid stress and indeed it would be unhealthy if we did. Stressors are motivating forces enabling us to sustain life and meet our needs, so without them we would fall sick or even die.

It is not stress, then, that we need to consider but rather *distress* which upsets our equilibrium and causes us so many problems.

All the information that we receive comes to us via our senses which screen for the ordinary and the out-of-the-ordinary. That screening takes place in the centre of our brain, an area known as the *hypothalamus*. If special action or response is called for the hypothalamus triggers the *pituitary* gland to respond and it produces the substance *adrenocorticotrophic hormone* (ACTH). ACTH activates two *adrenal glands* which sit one on top of each kidney. The outer layer of the gland secretes *sterocorticoids*, and the inner layer secretes *adrenalin* and *noradrenalin*. The combined effect of these substances as they circulate in the body causes the necessary physical changes which help us to deal with stress.

Let us take a familiar situation to illustrate the response. Suppose that, when you were young, you were unfamiliar with walking in the dark and you had occasion to move from a lighted area into a dark area. No doubt you felt a little frightened. If the breeze rustled the leaves of bushes around you, you might have thought that someone was in the shadows waiting to jump on you. As you were thinking these things your breathing started to go faster and your heart and pulse rate increased. You broke out into a sweat, felt cold and started to shiver. You were made ready to deal with the situation physically. Then you found your courage and moved from the dark to the light area once more. Almost instantly you felt relieved and within a short while your body chemistry was back to normal again. The causes and responses of stress are usually short-lived. For example, if you have an important interview or appointment you may keep wanting to empty your bladder or bowels. This is a normal response! The body is facing a crisis so it suspends some of its normal activities so that it can concentrate on responding to the stress situation.

This rising to the stressful occasion and fairly quickly returning to normal is described as a *transitory* emotional state. Health problems arise when, instead of the response subsiding, we remain in the responsive state, particularly over long periods of time. Our long-term exposure to the stress-response chemistry then becomes destructive rather than protective and contributes to a number of harmful conditions such as raised blood pressure, heart disease, diabetes and arthritis, to name but a few, and these may be acute or chronic conditions.

Perceptions

How we perceive any given situation is important since it will greatly affect our response. That is why people who work in emergency services have to practise and simulate the kinds of emergencies which they will have to deal with at some stage. As they become accustomed to emergency situations they are able to deal with these events with a professional detachment.

Life's experiences fit or condition us to respond in particular ways. That is why some people cope well and others appear to go to pieces. Our strengths and weaknesses are different because of our whole background, lifestyle and experience. Being able to see some experiences in a different light is obviously an advantage. We can, as it were, defuse some potentially explosive situations and avoid distress.

Stress-proofing

As we have seen, we cannot avoid stress, nor is it entirely desirable, so what measures can we take that will enable us to be strong in the face of distress?

It should be no surprise to learn that a balanced diet and regular exercise are our greatest helps. The Romans were fond of reminding the people that a sound mind exists in a sound body. Specifically we need to use foods that provide vitamin B to service our nervous system, and vitamin C to boost our immune system. We should avoid, as far as possible, sugars as they use up vitamin B as part of their metabolism in the body. Avoiding the use of alcohol, cigarettes and other drugs will help to protect the healthy state of the brain.

Different stressors will require different mental and psychological responses so we may have to find particular techniques for dealing with them. Highly stressed individuals should read up on or attend a stress management seminar in order to learn appropriate responses to meet individual needs, and all of us should recognize the symptoms of stress in our lives and practise a relaxation technique. In this way we can minimize the harmful effects of stress. It is also good to talk over our anxieties with a trusted friend. There are many times when we are so confused we just do not know what to do. Talking it through with someone helps us to put a focus on our thoughts and feelings, so making things a little clearer in our minds.

Do not forget the spiritual dimension. A sound faith helps us to stand against adverse circumstances that arise. The ongoing role of prayer helps to bring peace of mind wherever we might be. Associating with friends of like belief can be a strong support and help us through difficult times. We, in turn, can be an encouragement to others.

Stress affects many different people in many different ways.

Bible guidance in various experiences of life

Anger: Ephesians 4:25-32; James 3:1-18

Citizenship: Romans 12:17-13:14; 1 Peter 2:13-17

Conceit: Luke 18:9-14; Philippians 2:3-11

Contentment: Hebrews 13:5, 6

Crime: Matthew 15:19, 20; 1 Corinthians 6:9, 10

Death: John 11:25-27; 1 Thessalonians 4:13-18

Friendship: John 15:9-17; 1 Corinthians 15:33

Good Character: Galatians 5:22, 23; Philippians 4:8, 9

Greed: Luke 12:13-21; 1 Timothy 6:6-10

Hatred: Matthew 5:43-48; John 15:18-25

Hope: 1 Peter 1:3-9; 1 John 3:1-3

Humility: Luke 22:24-27; 1 Peter 5:5, 6

Love: 1 Corinthians 13:1-13; 1 John 4:7-21

Marriage: Mark 10:2-13; Ephesians 5:21-33

Obedience: Romans 13:1-7; James 1:22-25

Parents: Matthew 15:3-9; Ephesians 6:1-3

Patience: Hebrews 10:36-39; James 5:7-11

Permissiveness: Romans 6:1, 2, 11-14; 1 Corinthians 6:12-20

Purity: 2 Timothy 2:22; Titus 1:15, 16

Revenge: Matthew 5:38-42; Romans 12:17-21

Riches: Matthew 6:19-24; 1 Timothy 6:7-11

Self-control: James 1:19-21; 2 Peter 1:5-9

Thankfulness: Luke 17:11-19; 1 Thessalonians 5:16-18

Thoughts: Romans 8:5-8; Philippians 4:8

Where to find help in the Bible when:

Afraid or fearful: Matthew 10:26-31; Philippians 4:4-7; Psalm 34:1-8

Anxious or worried: Matthew 6:25-34; John 14:1-4; Psalm 46

Bereaved: 1 Corinthians 15:51-57; 1 Thessalonians 4:13-18; Psalm 23

Bitter or critical: Matthew 18:21, 22; Romans 2:1-4; Psalm 73:1-6, 21-28

Choosing a career: 1 Thessalonians 4:11, 12; James 4:13-15

Conscious of sin: Luke 7:36-50; 1 John 1:8-10; Psalm 51

Contemplating marriage: Matthew 19:4-6; Ephesians 5:22-33

Dedicating your life: Matthew 16:24-26; Romans 12:1, 2

Depressed or discouraged: Romans 8:28-39; 1 Peter 5:7

Doubting: Mark 9:23, 24; John 20:24-29

Failure comes: Hebrews 4:14-16; Jude 24, 25; Psalm 77:1-3, 10-15

Faith is weak: Luke 12:22-31; Hebrews 11

Far from God: Luke 15:11-24; Acts 17:22-30; Psalm 42:5-11

Feeling inadequate: 2 Corinthians 12:9, 10; Philippians 4:12, 13

Friends fail you: Luke 17:3, 4; 2 Timothy 4:16-18; Psalm 27:10-14

Ill or in pain: Luke 7:1-10; 2 Corinthians 12:9, 10; Psalm 103:1-4

In danger: Mark 4:37-41; Hebrews 13:6; Psalm 91:1-10

Leaving home: Hebrews 11:8-10; Luke 15:11-32

Lonely: John 14:15-21; Revelation 3:20; Psalm 23

Needing assurance: John 15:9-17; 1 John 3:19-24

Needing guidance: John 16:12, 13; James 1:5, 6; Psalm 32:8-10

Needing peace: Romans 5:1-5; Philippians 4:4-7

Needing sleep: Matthew 22:28; Psalm 4

Praying: Luke 11:1-13; John 14:12-14

Sad: 2 Corinthians 1:3-11; Revelation 21:1-5; Psalm 43:5

Tempted: 1 Corinthians 10:12, 13; James 1:12-15; Psalm 1

Wanting courage: Acts 4:13-31; Ephesians 6:10-20

Weary: Matthew 11:28-30; 2 Corinthians 4:16-18; Psalm 116:5-14

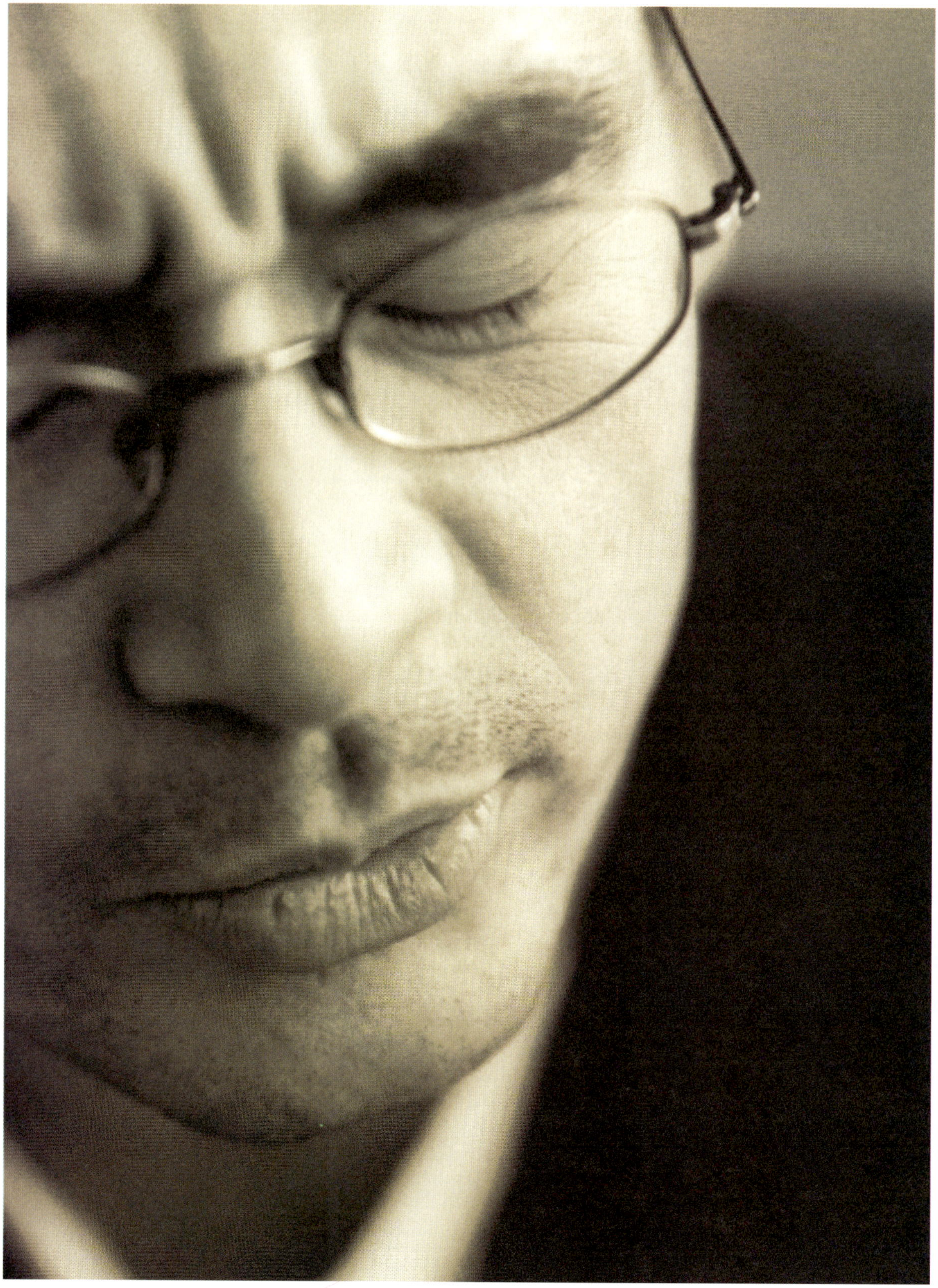

How to help your Mental Health

Mental Health

Mental health is as important as physical health and to a great degree depends on it. The brain requires some of all the nutrients that our food provides in order to function well. Even with the finest diet there can still be problems with the brain that affect our mental health. In the UK a study showed that 25 per cent of the over-85s develop dementia; and 10-16 per cent of the over-65s clinical depression.

Wherever we live we will always find mental illness in one form or another. It is important to note that there is a distinct difference between mental defects and mental illness. Mental defects are handicaps resulting from congenital diseases (usually acquired at birth) or genetic problems which leave the brain or intelligence impaired in some way. Mental illness may be a disorder arising from our feelings or emotions. Such illnesses may be found in otherwise healthy persons. Whatever the cause, we should not feel embarrassed or ashamed as these conditions are a natural part of the life that we lead. Usually they pass quite quickly and we can enjoy total health.

Talking Things Over

It helps to bring our problems out in the open. Sometimes our anxieties overwhelm us and we may see no way out of our difficulties. When we are undergoing great stress we can easily become muddled in our thinking. Just talking about our problem to a sympathetic friend helps to clarify our thoughts and place our difficulties in perspective.

When we realize that others have similar experiences to ours and are able to sort out their lives, we can be encouraged that our difficulties can be resolved also.

If we bottle up our feelings and do not give ourselves the opportunity to experiment with solutions to the stresses that we face, we may feel that we have let ourselves down and become even more depressed. We may try to isolate ourselves from the cause of the worry. Often in the process we isolate ourselves from family members or friends who might well be able to help us, even neglecting our appearance and adding to our woes. Many people who have mental sickness feel useless, inadequate and insecure. Being able to talk about our difficulties before they become a burden can be a great relief.

Signs of Mental Illness

The signs of mental illness may include the following:

- irritation and anger, with the person shouting or fighting for no obvious reason;
- unaccustomed rudeness;
- refusing to speak or eat;
- neglect of appearance, perhaps not washing or working;
- absenteeism;
- running away from home;

- no longer talking normally, but saying strange things;
- distant, faraway look in the eyes;
- no longer knowing or caring where one is, or what one is doing;
- seeing things or hearing voices that others present are not able to see or hear;
- wanting to fight with everyone;
- starting to drink more than usual, or seeking other drug relief.

Helping the Mentally Ill

Many of these characteristics, if recognized early, can be helped by good food, rest and talking things over. Some people will benefit from receiving professional help and/or medication until their difficulties have passed.

Where it is thought advisable, for reasons of safety or for availability of more intense treatment, individuals will be placed in hospital for short- or long-term care.

On return to the community, someone who has been in hospital will benefit from the care of family and friends. Acceptance in the community is very important and every effort should be made so that the person will feel the friendship and welcome of those around him or her. He or she must become active once more in the activities of the home, work, and community. Recent research shows clearly that belonging to groups and clubs can reduce health risks and help a person stay healthy. In fact, belonging to a church or holding a strong faith is the best protection of all. Any medicines prescribed on discharge from hospital must be taken to ensure no relapse.

Each of us can improve the mental health in our community by:

- being willing to listen (and perhaps talk) when we see people that we know having problems;
- helping the mentally ill and seeing that they get the right treatment;
- looking after the elderly around us, especially those who might already be having difficulty remembering;
- encouraging children to be at ease in discussing sensitive issues;
- helping and guiding children with learning or other difficulties, and by supporting their parents who may have difficulties in coping.

Dealing with a Crisis

Some people who have mental illness do not realize that they can get help for their condition. A small percentage of the mentally sick may cause disturbance from time to time. It helps to recognize that it is not the individual but, rather, the condition that is causing the problem. Talk gently and kindly to such people so as not to overexcite them by responding heatedly. Try to get them to a quiet place where you can talk and arrange for them to receive the necessary professional help.

There is no reason why mental illness should be regarded as being any different from other illness. As with any illness the sooner it is recognized the better the outlook for the person concerned. With prompt and appropriate treatment and care, the harmony of the home, workplace, and community may be restored.

How to help your Mental Health 45

Reducing Environmental Risks

Unhappy at Work

It would appear that most people are unhappy with some aspect of their work environment. Over 25 per cent of people in one study said that they had a stressful atmosphere in their workplace. Others complained of lack of desk space, the office location, not having others working around them or nowhere to meet their colleagues during a break.

While many of the stresses are minor and rank only as irksome, most people would put up with these so long as they had a job and an income. The real problems arise when these two major needs are not met.

Out of Work

Various studies have shown that there is an increase in ill-health when people face the prospect of unemployment. Fear of the unknown brings on all sorts of aches and pains and the anxieties that affect mental as well as physical health.

Worldwide studies show that a rise in unemployment leads to a corresponding increase in attempted, and successful, suicide; murders and prison convictions; psychiatric admissions; cirrhosis of the liver mortality; cardiovascular and general mortality rates. One of these studies showed that it may take up to three years for heart disease to manifest itself in the individuals concerned and persist for the next fifteen years regardless of whether or not employment has been found during that period. Another study showed that the partners and family of individuals made redundant are also at increased risk of ill-health.

People in low-paid jobs or jobs of short duration, with their consequent move from job to job, pay with their health. Health behaviours change as a result of recession or low pay. People are a lot less likely to eat well or to take regular exercise. As a result of despair in the face of overwhelming odds there is likely to be greater tobacco, alcohol and other drug use. The long-term effect of these behaviours may result in bronchitis, heart and lung disease, accidents, and low birth-weight babies.

Out of Home

Even worse than being out of work is the loss of one's home. Flood, fire, famine and war have contributed to vast numbers of people finding themselves in this situation. Understandably, there is an increase in health problems too, made worse by lack of access to medical facilities and attention.

Sleeping rough and having little regular and nourishing food adds musculoskeletal and respiratory problems to the individual's burdens along with schizophrenia and skin disorders. Very often the personal circumstances are so out of control that, with the best will in the world, they cannot be remedied.

Alleviating the Stress

In the work context we may well have to put up with the minor irritations that nag us from day to day. Where adjustments can be made to the benefit of all concerned these should be implemented.

Reducing Environmental Risks   **47**

We may not be able to control the factors surrounding our employment but enhancing our skills while we have the opportunity is a good idea. With a wider range of skills we may be more employable. Studies show that unemployed individuals who, instead of giving up, continue to do something at home similar to the work they had, do manage to offset some of the health problems. Living a life with a healthy routine while in work may also go a long way to maintaining health when difficult times come.

Where possible, some financial provision needs to be made for the future. Even if it is not a lot, it may help to cushion some of the immediate effects of unemployment.

As we have seen, it may not be possible to do anything about the natural disasters that come along. Aid is usually available at some stage and if this is rationed out it will help until circumstances change for the better. Good personal hygiene will help to reduce the risk of infection.

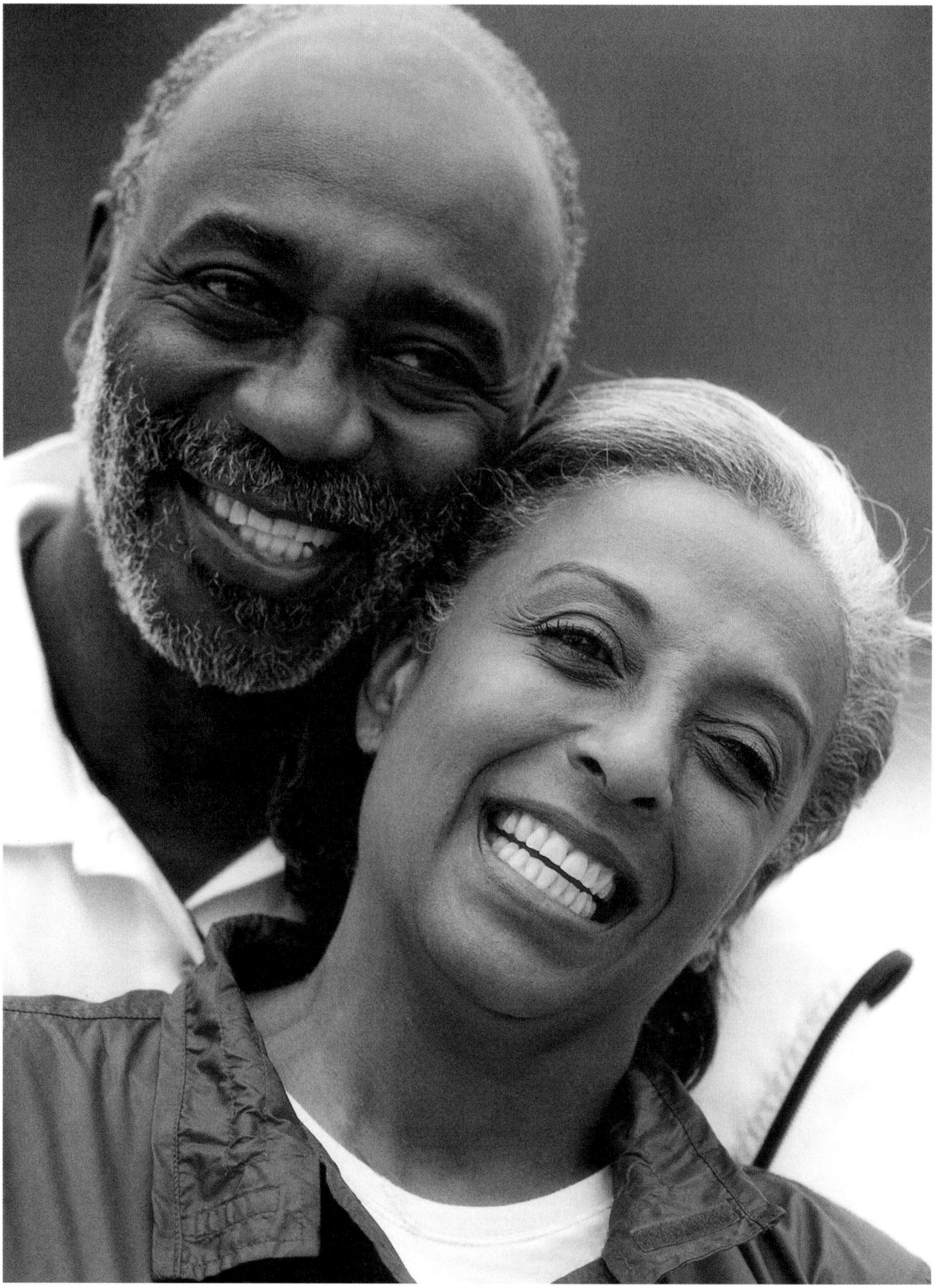

Reducing the Effects of Ageing

There is an air of optimism among the scientists studying ageing. By practically applying their findings, at our present level of knowledge, it is said that we could live to 120 years instead of the expected three-score-years-and-ten. It has been estimated that if we could keep throughout life the resistance to stress, injury and disease that we had at age 10, the majority of us might live to be more than 700 years old!

Meanwhile, our life expectancy has been stretched beyond the 70 years regarded as the norm by one of the writers of the biblical Psalms. What is encouraging here and now is that the older you are – the longer you live. If you are:

✦ 40 you can expect to live another 32.6 years = 72.6
✦ 45 you can expect to live another 28.3 years = 73.3
✦ 50 you can expect to live another 24.1 years = 74.1
✦ 60 you can expect to live another 16.8 years = 76.8

Many people are living well beyond these years.

The Paradox of Ageing

It's all very well living longer but longer is not necessarily better. So it is quality of life that counts. There have been some outstanding examples of longevity throughout the world. People in Ecuador, the Caucasus and the Hunza people of Pakistan have been widely reported as people who live longer and enjoy a high quality of life. Their secret is reputed to be a balanced diet, regular work and exercise, plenty of sleep and a laid-back approach to stress. While an average of 22 males and 50 females in 100,000 make their century in the UK, the Ecuadorans manage 100 out of 100,000. What has become apparent from all the research is that our chronological age is not usually the same as our biological age. Herein lies the paradox, some people are younger, say, at 55 than others at 45! Dr Harold Shryock says of such individuals that, except for serious accidents or major diseases, the youthful 55 will live longer than the 45-year-old who is already 'old'.

Why do we Age?

Obviously a number of factors can contribute to the ageing experience apart from the passage of time. These factors can be grouped under two main headings:

Intrinsic (inherited factors)
✦ Gerontologists (people who study ageing) have estimated that we have a body clock of approximately 7,000 genes with another 7,000 more peripherally involved. The chromosomes of these genes shorten with age and lose their ability to replicate and thus restore body cells. This process is slower in women hence they have a tendency to live longer.

  ✦ So, the production of a growth factor gradually declines;
  ✦ More ageing substances are produced;
  ✦ Growth ceases and cells that have been destroyed are not replaced;
  ✦ Cells malfunction;
  ✦ Harmful substances gradually accumulate in the cells.

Extrinsic (environmental factors):
✦ Injuries resulting from physical trauma, chemical or temperature changes;
✦ Diseases;
✦ Hazards associated with background and other radiation (either domestic or industrial);
✦ General interaction and reaction from day to day thus creating a hostile environment.

The Effects of Ageing

As the above intrinsic and extrinsic factors assail us we might expect that we will experience a range of physical and mental effects. These are put down to 'normal' changes that come with age. They include effects on all of the body systems and will vary from person to person:

- *body composition*. There is a tendency to decrease in muscle mass, especially if the person does not take regular exercise, and to increase in body fat. This leads to a loss of physical strength and power, impairs mobility, and increases the risk of disease.
- *body flexibility*. The stresses of the years begins to tell on the joints and there is increased stiffness of the connective tissue. This results in general body stiffness; loss of flexibility, joint stability and mobility.
- the *bones* change *their structure*. There is a decrease in bone minerals (*osteoporosis*, speeded up if drinks containing caffeine are used) with resulting increased risk of fracture, loss of height, or curvature of the spine.
- *cardiovascular system*. There is a decreased elasticity of blood vessels; decrease in heart muscle and volume; and a decrease in the electrical stimulation of the heart. These lead respectively to an increase in blood pressure; a decreased oxygen-carrying capacity; and a decrease in maximum heart rate.
- *respiratory system*. A decrease in the condition of the lung and its support structures makes hard work of breathing.
- *nervous system*. The speed at which nerve impulses

travel declines, thus making the person a little slower in responding to stimuli. Change in brain chemistry may cause inappropriate responses and/or confusion and memory loss, made worse by any existing damage to specific parts of the brain.

All the above may seem like a catalogue of woes, but keep in mind that they are not inevitable nor will all of these things happen for the vast majority of the ageing population.

Slowing the Ageing Process

It is not necessary to go on a search for the elusive fountain of youth in order to add quality to the years of life. There are, however, many simple measures that will help the person continue to enjoy a full life and a vigorous one. Activity arrests ageing. That is both physical and mental activity.

Social networks are also important in reducing the risks that can come with ageing. A considerable amount of research worldwide has shown that if a person is isolated, or perhaps perceives themselves as isolated, then their risk rate of a variety of conditions is raised. Being involved and active, on the other hand, increases protective hormones in the body.

Other factors which help to slow the ageing process include:

- a balanced diet. As body energy needs decrease with age, eating 5 per cent less each decade will help to keep the individual at an ideal weight. Eating a balanced diet will reduce the possibility of bone mineral loss;
- avoiding excessive fatigue by taking rest as it is needed;
- having a good exercise programme. This will help the respiration and heart, and also keep a good bone structure;
- as far as possible avoiding stress, and practising a good relaxation technique;
- having regular physical examinations.

If these good health practices are established much earlier in life – the sooner the better – then the transition through the ages will be less noticeable. Remember: We are today and tomorrow what we were yesterday and the day before – only more so!

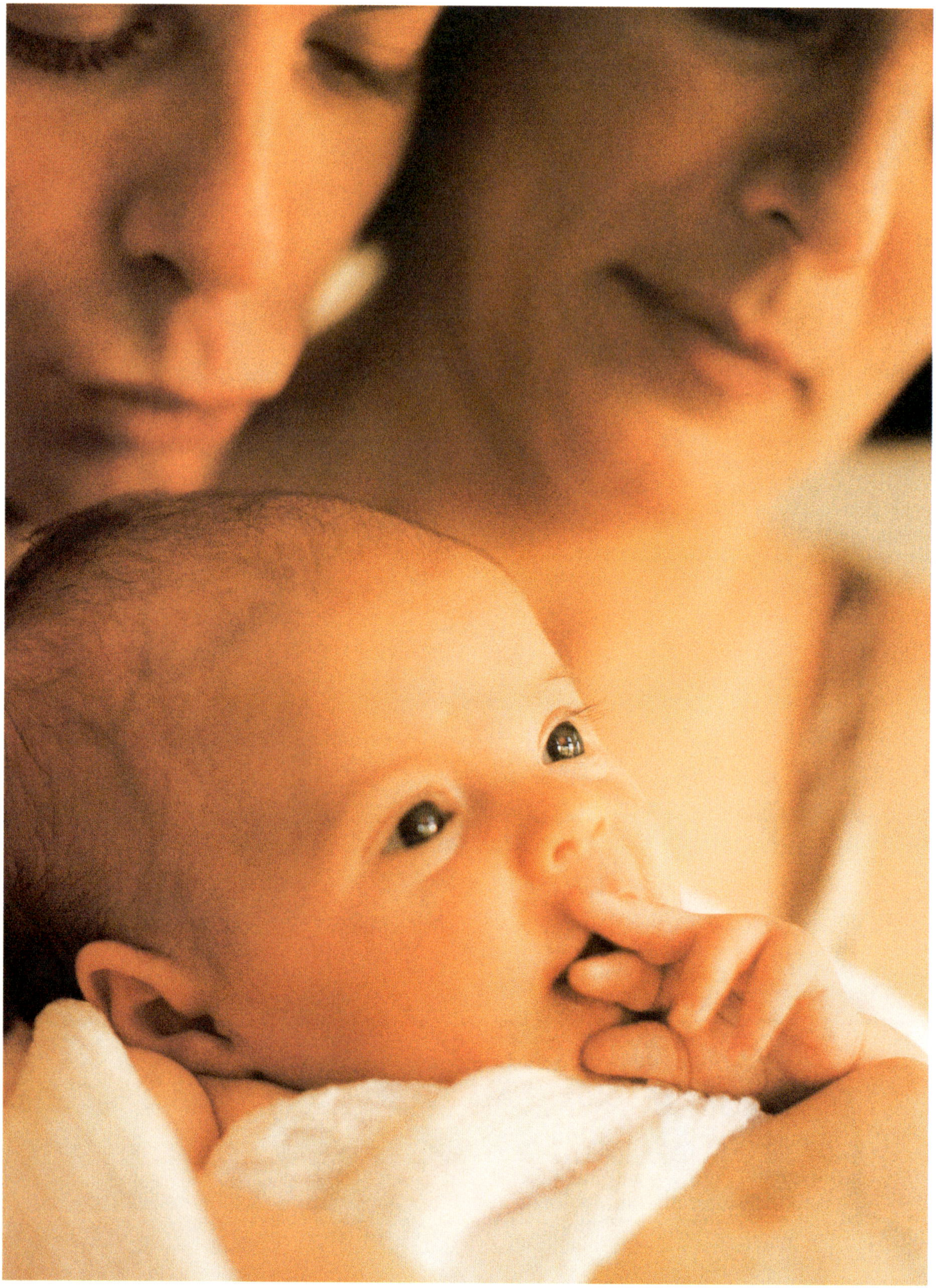

How to have a Healthy Pregnancy

Even if a woman has not been pregnant before, she is often aware of the fact before her pregnancy is confirmed, and the anticipated birth is an occasion for joy for most women.

The following are all normal signs of pregnancy:

- Missing a period – for many women the first sign;
- Nausea and the urge to vomit (morning sickness) occurring, as the name suggests, mostly in the morning. This may be worse in the second and third months;
- The belly enlarges;
- Frequency of urination;
- Breasts get bigger;
- Darker areas of pigmentation on the face, breasts and belly, referred to as the 'mask of pregnancy';
- During the fifth month the baby begins to move in the womb.

Staying Healthy in Pregnancy

All the principles of good health enjoyed from day to day need to be maintained during pregnancy so that the developing foetus may have a good start to life.

During this time of physical change, and perhaps uncertainty (if it is the first baby), it is most important to observe the following points:

- See the doctor or maternity nurse regularly and don't be afraid to ask questions or share any concerns;
- Remember to eat well. With an adequate well-balanced diet it is not necessary to 'eat for two'. However, eating the right kinds of food to provide proteins, vitamins and minerals (especially iron) benefits both of you. Try to keep sugars and salt to a minimum thereby avoiding excessive weight gain and possible water retention;
- *If you are a smoker or take alcohol and have not quit before pregnancy stop using these items right away;*
- Maintain good oral and body cleanliness. Brush your teeth after eating and bathe or wash regularly. Your breasts will be particularly important when the baby is born so will repay good care. Use a comfortable well-fitted brassiere for support and loose-fitting clothes for general comfort;
- Drink plenty of water and eat unrefined foods to avoid constipation and straining. Use only prescribed laxatives if needed.
- Avoid taking medicines unless they have been prescribed and are used under supervision. You may be advised to take vitamin or mineral supplements.
- Continue working for as long as you feel comfortable and try to get some regular exercise, particularly if work is not very physically demanding. Balance work and exercise with adequate amounts of rest and avoid getting too tired.
- As far as possible stay away from contact with measles (especially German measles) and any other infections.
- Enjoy sex for as long as you are comfortable and not endangering the womb.

Minor and Major Problems in Pregnancy

It is to be hoped that pregnancy will go smoothly. Indeed, in spite of inherent discomforts, many women seem to 'bloom' in pregnancy and enjoy the experience. As we don't live in an ideal world there may be some minor problems along the way.

These may include one or more of the following:

- *Anaemia and malnutrition.* Green leafy vegetables rich in iron and good protein foods should remedy this deficiency. Women already suffering these conditions before pregnancy will be prescribed supplements;

- *Burning or pain associated with 'heartburn' (acid indigestion).* Eating small amounts of food at a time and therefore more frequently will help to overcome indigestion difficulties. Use antacids only if advised to do so as part of your maternity care;

- *Constipation* (dealt with in the above section) may be severe. Use only prescribed laxatives as laxatives will deplete the body of vital nutrients;

- *Low back pain* due to the position of the womb and increasing weight of the baby. Exercise and standing or sitting with the back straight may help to ease discomfort;

- *Nausea or vomiting,* although a normal part of pregnancy, may be extremely unpleasant in the second and third months. It may be advisable to eat smaller meals during this phase; nibble on dry bread or crackers and avoid fatty foods;

- *Piles (haemorrhoids),* similar to varicose veins, but occurring in the anal veins resulting from the weight of the baby in the womb. The pain can be relieved by crouching with the bottom raised. Haemorrhoid creams can be obtained from the maternity centre;

- *Swelling of the feet* can best be avoided by resting as needed and putting the feet up. Eat less salt and salty foods and seek medical advice as the swelling comes from the pressure of the baby in the womb. Swelling is more common in anaemic and malnourished women and women using large amounts of salt;

- *Varicose veins.* This backward flow of blood in the legs is the result of the baby pressing on and restricting the flow of blood from the legs. Putting the feet up as often as you can will ease the swelling. If the swelling persists or the legs get particularly painful an elastic bandage will give the legs some support. Bandages should be taken off at night.

Minor problems are relatively easy to overcome. A small minority of women may have to face some major difficulties. Prompt recognition of these conditions and early treatment of the following special risks may help to lessen their impact:

Bleeding

- Bleeding, no matter how little, is **a danger sign** indicating a probable miscarriage.
- **Send someone for medical aid and lie quietly.**
- If the bleeding is occurring late in the pregnancy try to get to hospital **immediately**. Delay might prove fatal.

General Swelling

- Swelling of hands, feet and face accompanied by dizziness, headache and/or blurred vision or convulsions are signs of sudden weight gain, high blood pressure, and large quantities of protein in the urine.
- **Get medical advice right away.**
- Rest until help arrives and avoid the use of salt.

Severe Anaemia

- General tiredness, weakness, with pale or transparent skin.

- **Send for medical assistance.** The condition will probably need correction in hospital as a change of diet at this late stage will not remedy the problem.

Where possible try to make arrangements for the baby's birth near to the place where medical help and maternity care is available, or in a health centre or hospital, especially if there is a history of birth complication or you suspect that your labour may give you problems.

Keeping Track of Baby

- To calculate the expected date of birth, start with the date your last menstrual period began, then subtract three months from that date, and add seven days.

    For example: Last period began 30 August
    Take away three months = 30 May
    Add seven days = 6 June

To keep further track of your baby's progress as he or she grows in the womb, your womb will rise by the space of two fingers each month. At four and a half months your womb will be at the level of your navel (belly button).

The position of the baby in the womb is also important. Regular maternity checks will make certain that the baby is progressing in a normal manner.

From about five months the heartbeat and movement of the baby will be noticed, and become increasingly more recognizable as you near full-term.

Your maternity care team will keep you and the baby monitored and prepare you for the birth by explaining what will take place, and also teach you deep breathing which will assist you in the birth.

The happy moment arrives when you complete your healthy pregnancy and continue to practise and share your healthy lifestyle with your newborn child and integrate him or her into the wider care of the family.

How to Stay Healthy

Personal Lifestyle Factors

In the chapter HOW TO STAY HEALTHY we noted that lifestyle and environmental factors contributed to around 75 per cent of factors leading to death. It has also been emphasized in the other risk reduction chapters that maintaining health is an individual concern.

While we may have had the advantage of coming from a long line of healthy forebears, and even if we live in a healthy environment, we still need to concern ourselves with our personal health and care and develop a balanced lifestyle. Balance is the operative word as both neglect and excess in the various factors can bring problems in every area of life. Early faulty habits are a cause for later regret and may be hard to remedy.

Areas for Concern

Summarized, the main areas of consideration include the following:

Exercise
- necessary at all periods of life to develop and maintain a healthy body and mind, and to slow the effects of ageing;
- may be tailored to individual circumstances and capabilities;
- can be incorporated into our daily range of activities and be part of our family and other group activities.

Rest
- is needed on a regular basis for all the organs and systems of the body;
- reduces the impact of stress and may be taken in short sessions during the day as the opportunity arises, or as part of a fixed schedule of relaxational activity;
- can be suited to individual preference.

Sunlight
- aids the formation of vitamin D, through the action of ultraviolet light, which helps to build resistance to disease;
- kills harmful body bacteria by direct exposure.

Cleanliness

In addition to the above, personal cleanliness is of particular importance:

- *Cleanliness in general* – prevents build up of body parasites and bacteria by removing their breeding sites; removes dirt, perspiration and skin debris; protects against the spread of disease;
- Good *oral hygiene* protects against diseases of the mouth such as tooth decay and gum diseases, and some throat conditions;
- Keeping the ears and eyes clean protects these vital areas from becoming damaged and helps to ensure their prolonged use;

- Clean, well-fitting clothes and shoes will help the wearer to feel comfortable as well as preventing the growth of harmful bacteria.

Unhygienic Conditions

Later on, we note the role of an unhygienic environment in the spread of TB, but personal uncleanliness may lead to other conditions associated with food poisoning, infections, and worms.

- *Food poisoning* occurs as a result of germs being passed on to the digestive process of others when food handlers do not wash their hands and are careless in the food preparation environment. It is particularly important to wash the hands after going to the toilet, and to ensure that all work surfaces and kitchen equipment are kept clean.
- *Infections* such as **infective hepatitis** (jaundice) are spread by germs and are found all around the world but particularly in children and young adults. Infective hepatitis is one of a number of diseases affecting the liver:

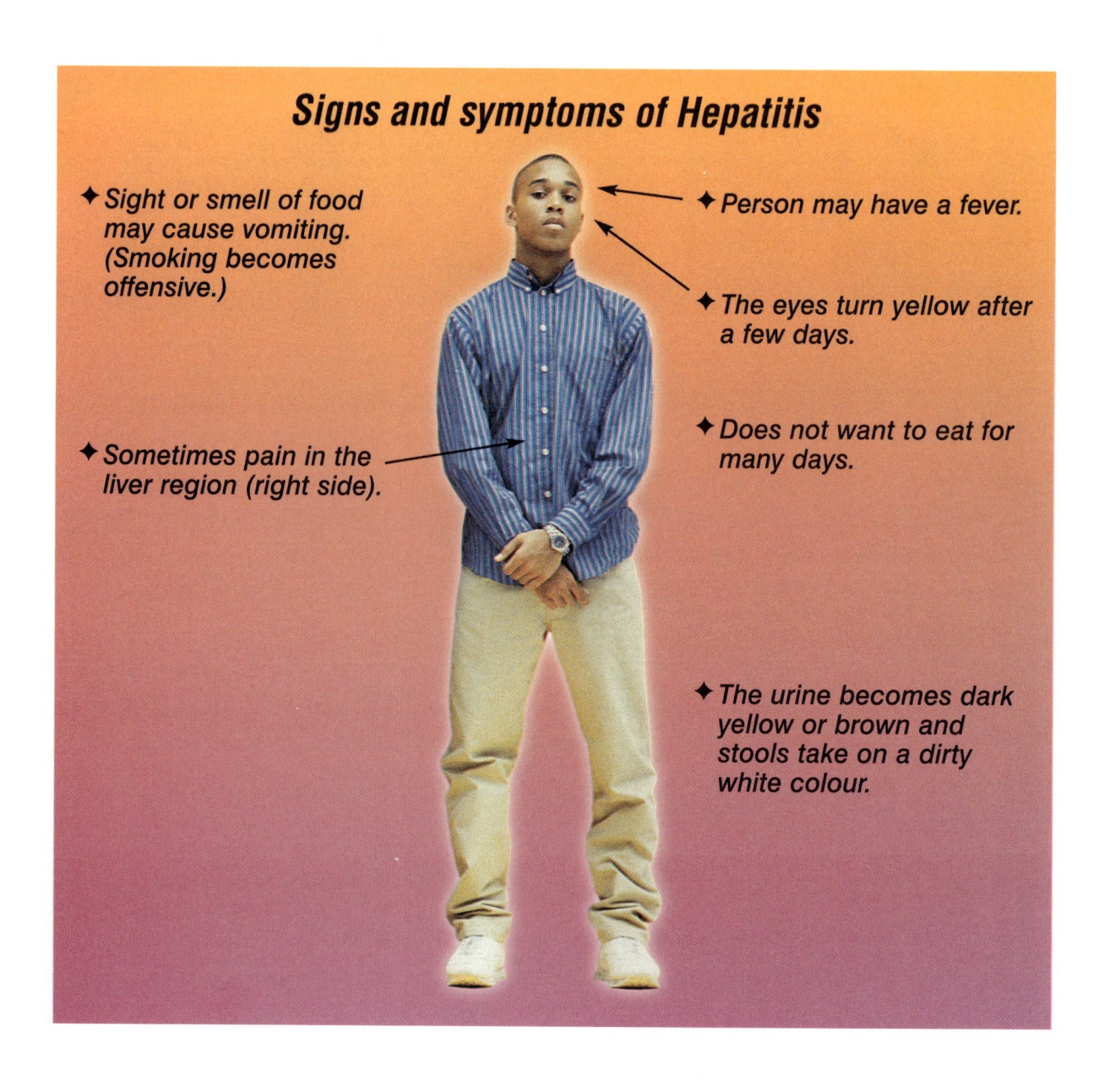

Signs and symptoms of Hepatitis

- *Sight or smell of food may cause vomiting. (Smoking becomes offensive.)*
- *Sometimes pain in the liver region (right side).*
- *Person may have a fever.*
- *The eyes turn yellow after a few days.*
- *Does not want to eat for many days.*
- *The urine becomes dark yellow or brown and stools take on a dirty white colour.*

Prevention and Treatment

- Good oral and body hygiene;
- In places without sanitation, infected stools must be buried, burnt or otherwise appropriately disposed of;
- The hands of any contacts with the infected person or their stools should be thoroughly washed;
- Use safe fluids and foods;
- Most of the signs disappear in 2-6 weeks without any particular treatment;
- Blood and liver function tests along with ultrasound scanning will determine what specific treatment is needed;
- Rest, only as required – complete bed rest is not necessary;
- Drink plenty of fluids and eat a well-balanced diet avoiding alcoholic drinks and fatty foods;
- Keep to any prescribed therapeutic regime.

Worms

- There are several different types of worms which can live in the human body –

  Pinworms *(threadworms)*
  Roundworms *(nemotodes)*
  Hookworms
  Tapeworms

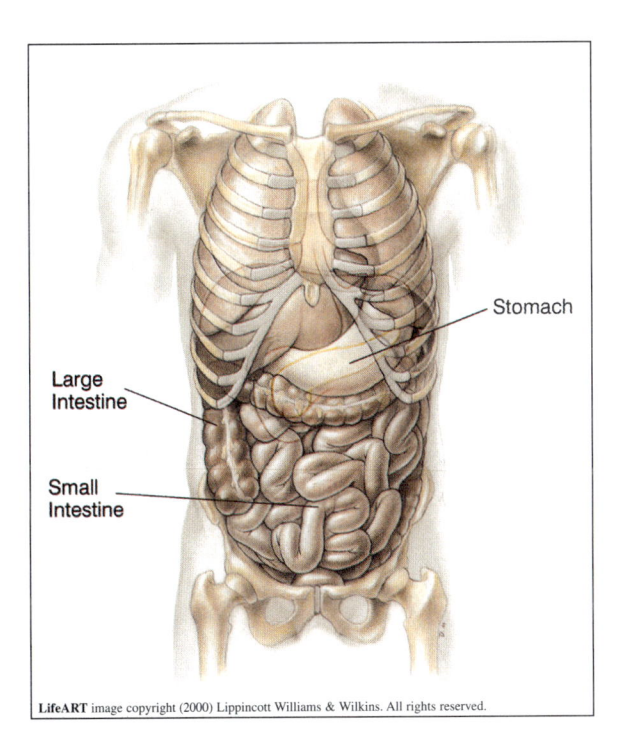

Good personal hygiene is the single most important factor in preventing infestation by worms.

Threadworms

- Worms live in the large intestine;
- Female worms migrate to anal region and lay eggs;
- Eggs are transferred to the mouth by handling contaminated material and poor personal hygiene;
- The cycle of infestation is repeated;
- Person experiences intense itching around the anal region, particularly at night.

Roundworms

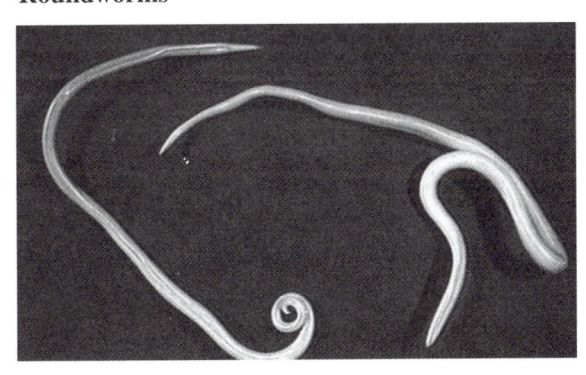

- Roundworm eggs are swallowed and hatch in small intestine and get into the bloodstream;
- May cause allergy-type itch and fever;
- Worms live in the intestines (female may lay 200,000 eggs a day);
- Worms travel in the body and may crawl in nose and mouth;
- Eggs may survive outside the body for months in moist, shady places;

+ The cycle is perpetuated by poor hygiene.

Hookworms

+ Larvae penetrate the skin of the feet or are ingested, so entering the bloodstream;
+ Worms migrate throughout the body, attaching themselves to the small intestine;
+ Worms develop to adulthood, lay eggs which are passed with the stools and finally hatch as larvae;
+ Person suffers stomach ache, and is pale and weak;
+ Worms may be coughed up and swallowed;
+ Poor hygiene perpetuates the cycle.

Tapeworms

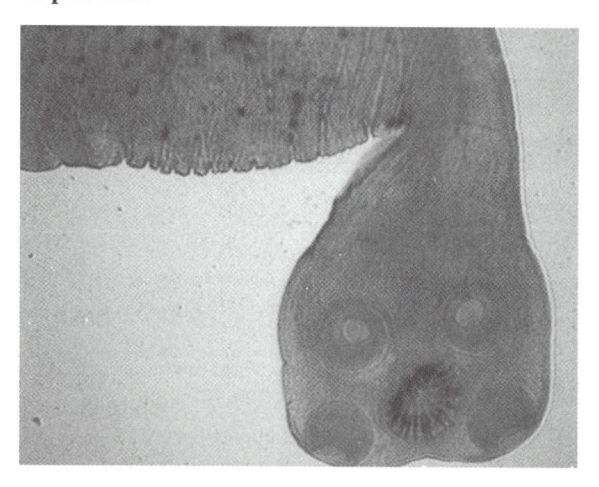

+ Vary in length from dwarf to 5 metres;
+ Made of small, flat white pieces which break off and are passed in the stool;
+ Pigs and cows eat the faecal matter thus becoming hosts to the parasites;
+ People eating undercooked pork and beef ingest worms which grow in the intestines;
+ Sometimes mild stomach ache, vomiting, or a change in the bowel habits;
+ More rarely, small cysts or sacs of baby worms migrate to the brain causing headaches, fits, and death;
+ Poor personal hygiene perpetuates the cycle.

Treatment

+ Good personal cleanliness, especially of the anal region and the hands. Keep fingernails well clipped and scrubbed;
+ Vaseline around anus to relieve itching;
+ Get medical advice promptly;
+ Use medication as prescribed;
+ Protect food from flies, etc, and keep all utensils and work surfaces in the kitchen as clean as possible;
+ Dispose of waste material carefully either by burning or burying;
+ Where meat is used ensure that it is well cooked.

Hygienic Routine

Establishing and maintaining a good hygienic routine personally and in the family will help to protect family and community members from a wide range of diseases and conditions, some of which may be mild in effect but others life-threatening. Simple measures may result in lives saved, and better quality of life for all concerned.

Personal Lifestyle Factors 61

How to Stop Smoking

For the person wanting to be physically fit, smoking – in all its forms – is bad news. Smoking is dangerous to your own health, to the health of your family, and to other people's health in the workplace or community. Most smokers are addicted to nicotine and may be both chemically and habitually dependent on their smoking habit.

The following points are specific to cigarette smoking but the principles set out can be used to quit pipe and cigar smoking and also chewing tobacco. The physical results of using tobacco other than in the form of cigarettes concentrates damage to other sites in the body.

Smoking Damage

Where cigarettes are part of the lifestyle the dangers of smoking are many and varied. They include:

- *Lung damage,* ranging from difficulties in breathing to bronchitis and lung cancer. Even allowing for other hazards to breathing that might be present in the community, the incidence of these lung conditions rises dramatically when a person smokes. One cigarette forces the lungs to do twenty per cent more work;

- *Damage to the stomach* by causing stomach ulcers or contributing to the problem where these are already present;

- *Heart and circulatory problems.* Nicotine constricts blood vessels all over the body and causes the heart to work harder. Just one cigarette makes the heart blood pressure rise (hypertension) for about nine hours. Continually smoking keeps the blood pressure raised and also forces cholesterol to circulate more freely in the bloodstream. Hypertension and high levels of cholesterol are both risk factors in heart disease;

- *Impairment of the brain,* by robbing the blood of oxygen and replacing it with harmful carbon-monoxide;

- *Damage to the unborn baby* by restricting the access of some essential nutrients through the placenta (where the maternal blood supply nourishes the developing foetus) possibly causing smaller babies and lower birth-weight. The susceptibility of the infant and the young child to various infections, diseases and conditions is also increased by maternal pre-birth smoking. This vulnerability follows the child through to the teen and early adult years;

- *Passive smoking problems* as others are forced to inhale 'secondhand' smoke. The effect is virtually the same as smoking directly but may take longer to develop;

- *The family food budget may be affected,* limiting the family's access to well-balanced nutrition. Some families budget for cigarettes, or other forms of smoking, before they budget for the needs of the family.

Quitting Smoking

The following ten steps may be useful for those who want to stop smoking. Millions of people around the world have been successful in quitting smoking by using these simple methods:

- *Know why you want to stop*

  Some people have a vague idea that smoking is not doing them any good, or that they are spending a lot of money. So take time to think through your personal reasons for quitting. Reasons may include health, finance, example to children, etc., but they must outweigh your reasons for continuing to smoke. It is good to write down your reasons and keep them close to help in your motivation.

- *Make a strong positive decision*

  No maybes. Definitely *choose* not to smoke. The speaking of the words 'I choose not to smoke', especially when there is craving, has proved to be useful to many people. Eventually the brain accepts your choice. Choosing not to smoke has the advantage of not being a resolution or a promise – you are merely exercising choice. If you do smoke in these early stages it is not necessary to feel shame or embarrassment, simply choose again not to smoke when the temptation comes along. Choosing exerts an effect on the physical and psychological processes.

- *Quit now*

  Don't put off your choice and don't set yourself up for failure by keeping cigarettes around 'just in case'. You may have a rough few days but if you are not putting nicotine into the system it is easier to get rid of what is already there. Peaks of craving come; but they only last for a few minutes at most. They also decrease in intensity and come less frequently as time passes. Just keep occupied through the craving time and then get on with the business of life. Try not to fight battles with craving ahead of time. Meet them as they come.

- *Eat wisely*

  What you eat and drink during your quitting programme is very important. There is, for example, a chemical relationship between nicotine and caffeine so it is wise to avoid anything with caffeine in it while you are struggling to overcome the craving. Take water or fresh fruit juices instead, or try herbal teas that give a different taste in the mouth.

  Eating fruits and vegetables, and avoiding meat dishes, will provide the alkaline or neutral body pH value (acid/alkaline balance) conducive to quitting.

Several recent studies support the idea that changing the body pH levels, by ingesting either acidifying or alkalinizing agents, influences smoking behaviour. The following partial list of food items are ranked according to their degree of acidity (-), or alkalinity (+). (Smoking favours an acid shift in the body that meat provides.)

Fruits and vegetables will also help to cleanse the body. Avoid all high calorie foods likely to contribute to weight gain. If you have to snack, then snack on raw vegetables. Keep the diet light for the

Body pH Levels

Foods that INCREASE withdrawal symptoms	Average	Foods that LESSEN withdrawal symptoms	Average
Egg yolks	- 27.00	Milk	+02.01
Beef	- 21.00	Apples	+03.07
Chicken	- 14.00	Bananas	+05.00
Oatmeal	- 12.00	Oranges, Tomatoes	+05.06
		Cabbages, Molasses, Brown Sugar	+06.00
Barley	- 11.00	Coconuts	+08.00
Rice	- 05.07	Broccoli (greens)	+09.03
Cheeses	- 05.00	Limes	+10.00
White Bread	- 04.00	Dates	+11.00
Peanuts, Pecans, Walnuts	- 03.00	Almonds	+12.00
Cranberries, Prunes	- 01.00	Tofu	+18.00
White Sugar, Oils	- 00.00	Beet Greens, Spinach, Squash	+27.00
		Lima Beans	+28.42
		Figs	+33.00
		Raisins	+34.00

first few days, gradually increasing it and adjusting to an otherwise healthy one.

✦ *Drink water*

Nicotine's one redeeming factor is that it is soluble in water. Drinking large quantities of water will help flush nicotine from the system. Once the nicotine has been washed out the physical craving is reduced.

Avoid alcohol (if alcohol is normally used) as it affects the decision-making part of the brain, thus sabotaging the exercise of choice.

✦ *Outside water*

Take more than your usual number of warm baths or showers during the first week of quitting smoking. The skin being an excretory organ will help to rid the body of nicotine.

✦ *Deep breathing*

Try deep breathing exercises, especially after meals. Spend as much time as possible outdoors and include some simple exercises to encourage a good oxygen intake. Go easy in the early stages, as you might feel light-headed and dizzy.

✦ *Keep a regular programme*

Eating, sleeping, exercising, and working are part of a familiar programme for the day. Too many changes can be disruptive and especially so when a major change such as stopping smoking is taking place. Regularity will help to establish good health habits.

✦ *Outside help*

Draw on your faith, and draw on your family. You need all the help that you can get. None of us is so strong that we can go it alone. Prayer may prove to be your greatest asset in the battle with self.

✦ *Don't quit quitting!*

Too many people give up at the least bit of hardship. That is why your reasons for quitting are so important. It is always darkest before the dawn so don't give up when things are rough. Millions of people have trodden a similar path to yours and discovered by persistence that victory is just around the corner. So give yourself a chance to succeed. If necessary, try and try again. The benefits are immediate [short and long-term], so there is much to look forward to.

Withdrawal symptoms

Some people stop smoking with relative ease, but for others it is a struggle, and for a few a major battle. Although you are not bound to experience withdrawal symptoms, the following are fairly common:

Aching muscles	Muscle twitching
Craving for food	Nausea
Craving to smoke	Spots before eyes
Exhaustion	Sweating/hands, body
Eye pain	Taste changes
Headache	Tiredness
Irritability	Trembling inside
Lack of concentration	Trembling of hands
Light-headedness/dizziness	Vomiting
Loss of appetite	Prickly sensation of skin

Many of these symptoms are associated with adjustments being made in the nervous system. Foods containing the B vitamins and vitamin C will help to offset these problems. These include: unrefined cereals, legumes, nuts, and potatoes for B vitamins; citrus fruits, peppers, potatoes, and rich green vegetables for vitamin C.

How to Stop Smoking 65

Reducing Alcohol and other Drug Risk

Curiosity

A sense of curiosity and peer group pressure lead many young people to experiment with alcohol and other drugs. The availability of many of these drugs encourages their wide use. People react to drugs in different ways, and adverse effects may put off many from further experimentation. However, many other people like the effect of drugs, particularly to enhance otherwise positive experiences, or to escape the rather deadly life that they live.

The effects of drugs can be listed under three main headings:

- *stimulants* – which fire up the nervous system, such as the caffeine in tea, coffee, cola drinks
- *depressants* – which dampen down or depress nervous reaction. Alcohol falls into this category
- *hallucinogenics* – which distort perception of time, space, reality, etc.

The use of these drugs on anything approaching a regular basis can lead to *psychological* or *physiological* addiction. Psychological addiction is the feeling that we cannot do without the drug. Physiological addiction results when physical withdrawal symptoms occur that are relieved by taking the same or similar drugs. (See chart on page 68 to see which drugs have which effects.) Apart from withdrawal problems, drugs may do permanent damage to the body or brain.

Spotting Drug Use

There are a number of signs in the home which might indicate the use of alcohol or other drugs. These include:

- sudden changes of mood in the individual with unusual irritability or aggression;
- loss of appetite;
- loss of interest in hobbies, sport, school-work or friends;
- unusual bouts of drowsiness or sleeping;
- furtive behaviour and telling lies to cover actions;
- unexplained loss of money or saleable objects;
- unusual smells on the breath or the person, stains or marks on the body, the clothes, or around the house;
- hidden bottles, unusual powders, tablets, capsules, scorched tinfoil, needles or syringes.

Warning signs of alcohol or other drug use in the workplace include:

- person less good at job;
- poor time-keeping;
- ill more often than usual;
- dishonesty;

'Many people like the effect of drugs and alcohol, particularly to enhance otherwise positive experiences, or to escape the rather deadly life that they live.'

- sudden mood swings from pleasant to irritable, or even aggression;
- person becomes hard to get on with.

A pattern will emerge from these signs which will be evident in the sickness records, behavioural observations, and productivity of the individual concerned.

Getting Straightened Out

However carefully the suspicions are voiced the individual is likely to be aggressive and on the defensive. Unless the individual wants to quit the habit it will be difficult to effect change. A caring attitude may do much to break through the wall of hostility and a listening ear may help the person open up about their problem. Recognizing the problem is the first step to recovery, and laying plans for recovery which can be monitored for effectiveness are essential. The support of leaders in the faith community and people used to dealing with abuse problems will help to sort out difficulties in the home and the workplace. Depending on the nature and the severity of the problem, health care should be provided by either the doctor or nearest health facility.

Encouraging a drug-free approach to life will help the growing child see that life can be lived to its fullest without the crutch of drugs. Be accepting, especially where human frailties have become apparent, and surround family members with unconditional love and support. Try to do fun things together as a family.

Some common groups of drugs and their effects

GROUP/DRUGS	EFFECTS
STIMULANTS	
AMPHETAMINES (Uppers)	Excitability, rapid and unclear speech, restlessness, tremors, insomnia, sweating, dry mouth, bad breath, itchy nose, dilated pupils. Continued use results in increased pulse and blood pressure, hallucinations, psychoses.
CAFFEINE & NICOTINE	Excitability, tremors, palpitations increasing with quantity drunk/smoked.
CANNABIS (Marijuana) *Cannabis sativa*	Euphoria, dizziness, excitability, hallucinations, increased appetite, dryness of mouth, increased pulse and blood pressure, nausea.
DEPRESSANTS	
ALCOHOL	Slurred speech, uncoordination, unsteadiness, confusion, tremors, drowsiness, agitation, nausea, respiratory depression. Continued use can damage the liver and brain and enlarge and weaken the heart.
BARBITURATES (Downers)	Similar to alcohol intoxication, drowsiness, confusion, uncoordination, tremors. Continued use results in depressed pulse and blood pressure, possible convulsions.
COCAINE	Excitability, talkativeness, headache, nausea. Continued use results in increased blood pressure and pulse rate, possible hallucinations and violent or dangerous behaviour.
CODEINE	Drowsiness, pinpoint pupils, stupor, sometimes nausea develops. Continued use develops a tolerance to drug.
HEROIN, Crack	Relaxation, drowsiness, confusion, euphoria, slurred speech, flushing of skin on face, nausea, constricted pupils, respiratory depression. Continued use results in scars of abscesses at injection points.
MORPHINE	Lethargy, drowsiness, confusion, euphoria, slurred speech, flushing of skin, nausea, constricted pupils, respiratory depression. Continued use results in scars of abscesses at injection points.
HALLUCINOGENS	
DMT; LSD; MDMA (Ecstasy); Psilocybin; etc.	Trance, anxiety, confusion, tremors, euphoria, depression, dilated pupils, increased pulse rate and blood pressure. Continued use may result in psychoses, possible chromosomal breakdown and organic brain damage.
CANNABIS (Marijuana) *Cannabis sativa*	Euphoria, dizziness, excitability, hallucinations, increased appetite, dryness of mouth, increased pulse and blood pressure, nausea.
MESCALINE	Resembles LSD effects. Distortion of senses, anxiety, confusion, tremors, euphoria, depression, dilated pupils, increased pulse rate, psychoses, and possible hallucinations.
SOLVENTS	
(includes glue, paint thinner, petrol, etc.)	Similar to alcohol intoxication. Slurred speech, blurred vision, uncoordination, ringing in ears, nausea, and vomiting. Continued use results in psychoses, hallucinations, liver and blood damage, respiratory depression.

Positive alternatives to a drug lifestyle

FELT NEED	PRIME MOTIVATION	DRUG-FREE ALTERNATIVE
CREATIVE-AESTHETIC	To improve creativity; to further enjoyment of art, music, etc.	Attending concerts; taking courses in art, music, crafts, handiwork, writing, singing, etc.
EMOTIONAL	Attempt to solve personal problems; relief from bad moods; escape from anxiety; emotional relaxation.	Instruction in personal development; stress management and relaxation; competent counselling and therapy; artistic self-expression through painting, music, etc.
INTELLECTUAL	To escape mental boredom; to find solutions to intellectual problems; to study better.	Reading, debating, discussions; creative games and puzzles; training in concentration; memory training.
INTERPERSONAL	Acceptance among friends; desire to communicate with other people; to love and be loved.	Emphasis on assisting others in distress; group therapy; stronger family ties; friends of both sexes.
PHILOSOPHICAL	To discover meaningful values; to grasp the nature of the universe; to find the meaning of life.	Study of concepts of ethics, morality, and reality; family discussion; seminars; works of the great philosophers.
PHYSICAL	Desire for physical satisfaction: relief from sickness; desire for more energy; greater fitness.	Medical attention; healthier diet; exercise; more sleep and relaxation; sports; outdoor work or gardening.
SENSORY	Desire to stimulate sight, sound, touch, taste; for sensual experience; need for excitement.	Change of scenery; experiencing the sensory beauty of nature; exciting sports such as surfing, skiing or swimming.
SOCIOPOLITICAL	To promote social, political, legal, economic, and environmental change; to find an identity with society.	Study of pollution of the environment; community action and positive social change; helping the poor, aged, young, infirm; tutoring the handicapped.
SPIRITUAL-MYSTICAL	To transcend orthodox religion; to develop spiritual insight; to communicate with God; to reach higher levels of consciousness.	Christian meditation; Bible study; study of world religions; study of Christian theology; reading about great Christians.
MISCELLANEOUS	Adventure, risk, 'kicks'; unexpressed motives; pro-drug general attitudes.	Adventure activities such as 'Outward Bound' survival training; a mix of alternatives above; 'back-to-nature' attitudes; meaningful employment; youth work.

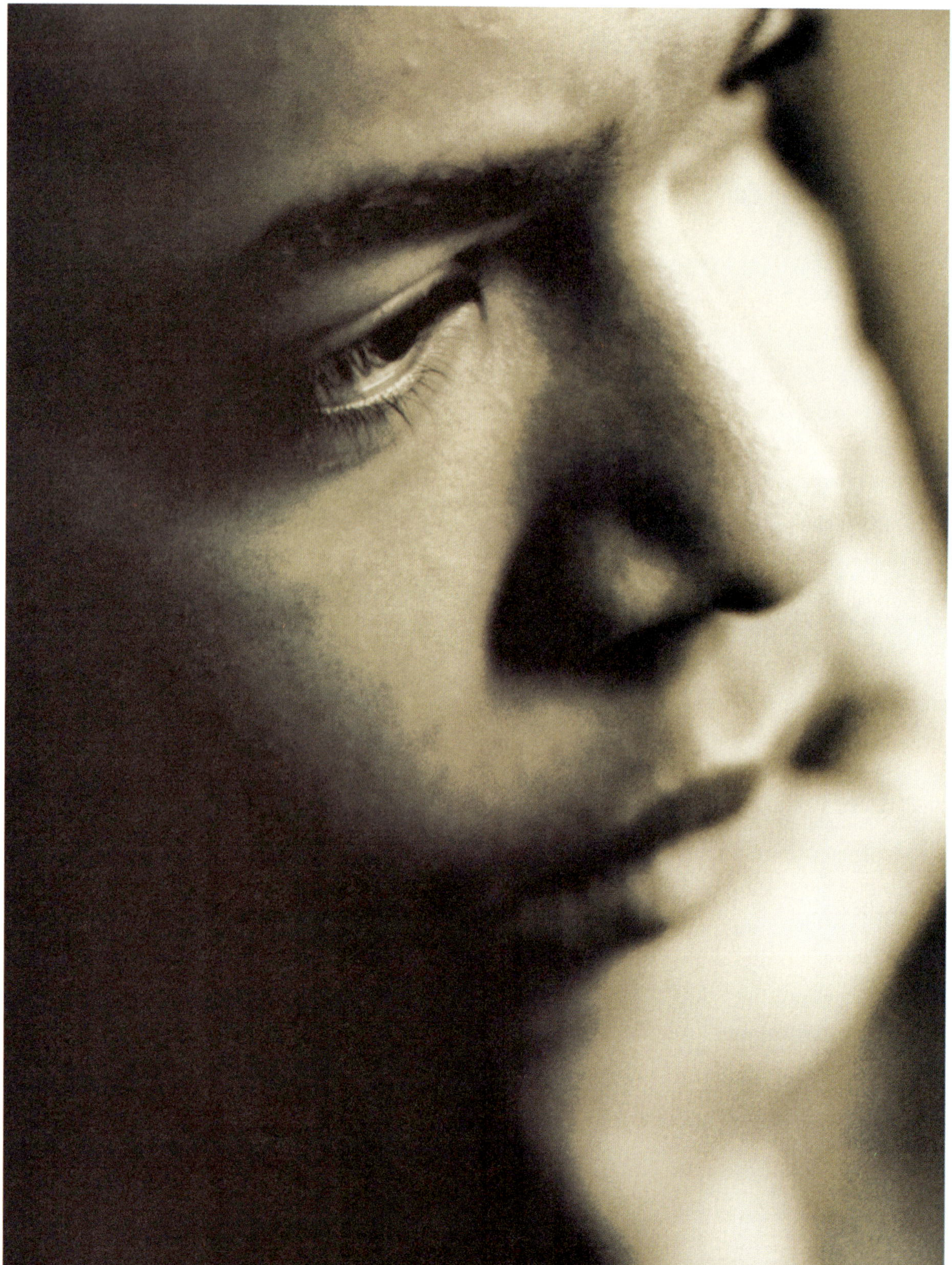

Reducing Tuberculosis Risk

Up to very recently, tuberculosis (TB) was the world's leading cause of death due to infectious disease. Until late in the 1980s there were about 6,000 new cases annually in the UK. It was thought to be virtually eliminated from Britain by the middle 1990s. Now there is a resurgence of the infection due to people coming over from other areas of the world where tuberculosis is still prevalent. People coming to the UK from the Indian subcontinent in particular now account for approximately one third of all new cases of tuberculosis diagnosed in Britain. The infection is around 25 times more common in these immigrants than in the indigenous population.

TB kills two million people every year. The World Health Organization estimates that between the years 2000 and 2020 there will be nearly one billion newly-infected people (every second adds one newly-infected individual worldwide); 200 million will get sick from TB; and around 35 million of those will die of the infection. Over 1.5 million cases per year of TB occur in sub-Saharan Africa.

Tuberculosis Infection

TB has been described as a disease of deprivation because it is commonly found among the most deprived people worldwide. The infection is caused by a bacterium – *mycobacterium tuberculosis* – and was a major cause of death in Western countries in times past. It particularly affected children and young adults:

- TB can 'attack' any part of the body but is usually associated with the lungs (a condition known as *pulmonary TB*). Life-threatening complications of pulmonary TB include:
  pneumothorax (air collecting between the lung and chest wall);
  pleural effusion (fluid collecting between the lung and chest wall).

- The TB bacillus is spread by the small droplets produced by sneezing and coughing, and they are inhaled by people nearby; and may also be ingested through contaminated food such as milk from tubercular cows.

- Often the voice-box *(larynx)* is affected, thus making a person's voice sound rough and deep.

- There will be – in the case of pulmonary TB – a progressive shortness of breath. This is accompanied by fever, particularly night sweats, and a loss of weight and strength.

- In addition to suffering the effects of deprivation, others may be at special risk. These include people suffering from *diabetes*, alcohol dependence, or disorders of the immune system *(immunodeficiency)*. So TB is spreading rapidly among people with AIDS.

- Detection of any of the above, or any of the following features, should be checked out as soon as possible. At the medical examination appropriate tests will establish a diagnosis.

Areas of the body that might be affected by tuberculosis

Tumours that might disfigure the face

Tuberculosis of the lymph nodes (scrofuloderma)

Tuberculosis of the lungs

Tuberculosis of the backbone

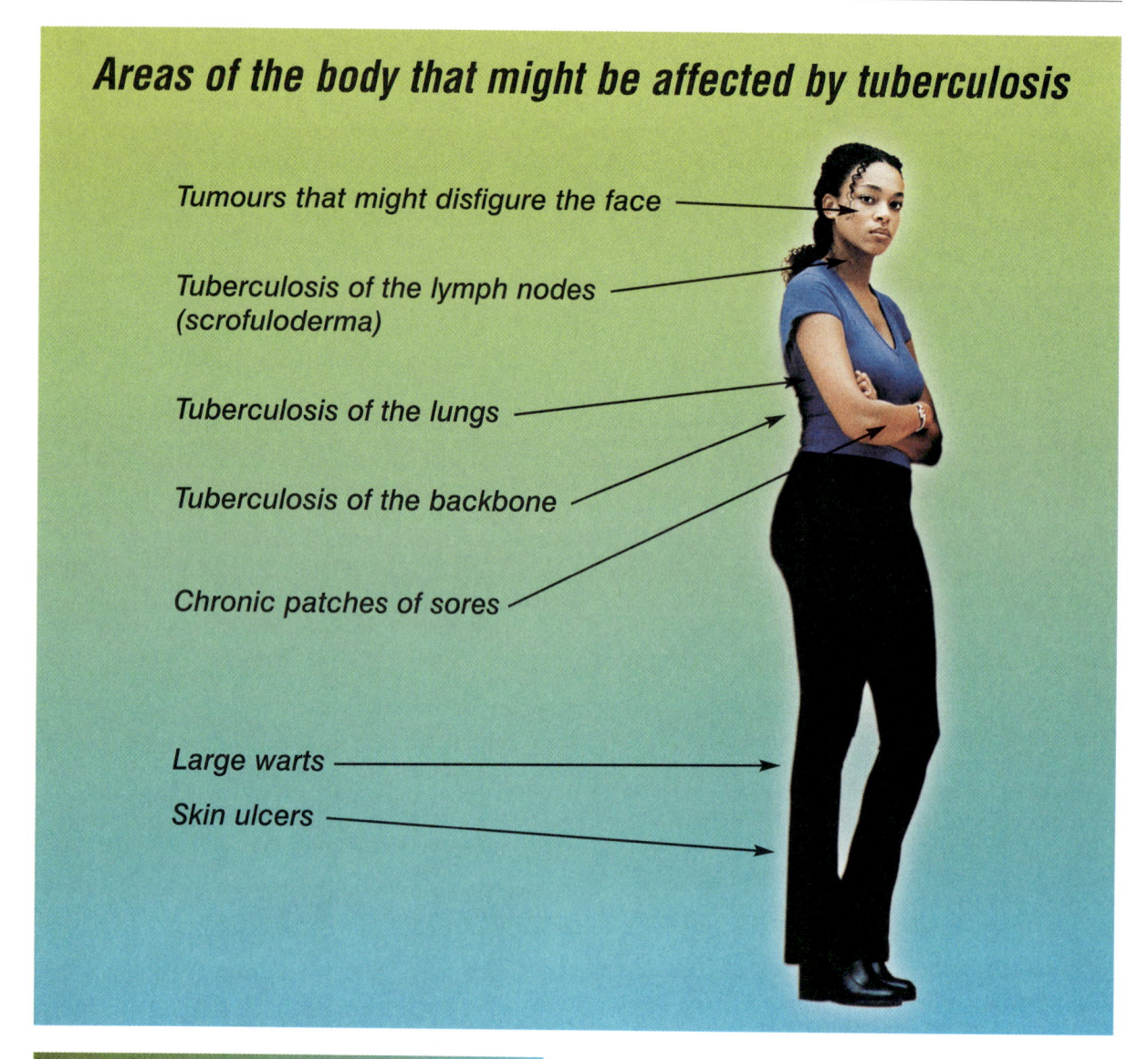

Chronic patches of sores

Large warts

Skin ulcers

Prevention and Treatment of TB

- Elimination, as far as possible, of the conditions under which TB thrives. These conditions include overcrowding, poverty-level living, and inadequate nutrition. The individual may not be able to do a lot to remedy these social ills;
- Good personal hygiene generally and especially when coughing and sneezing, and when other forms of tuberculosis are present;
- Early BCG *(Bacillus Calmette-Gurin)* vaccine. The vaccine may be used in either of two ways:
  - Protecting newly-born babies or children at particular risk of infection;
  - Immunization of young adults or at-risk groups in the community.
- Keeping children in particular away from risk situations;
- The use of sterilized milk, and of pasteurized dairy products;
- Chemotherapy as prescribed, with periodic blood tests to rule out any damage to the liver as a result of the medications used;
- Compliance with the prescription instruction usually means that upon completion of the course of medication the individual is considered cured and is unlikely to have a recurrence of the condition;
- Contact tracing so that risk to others may be minimized.

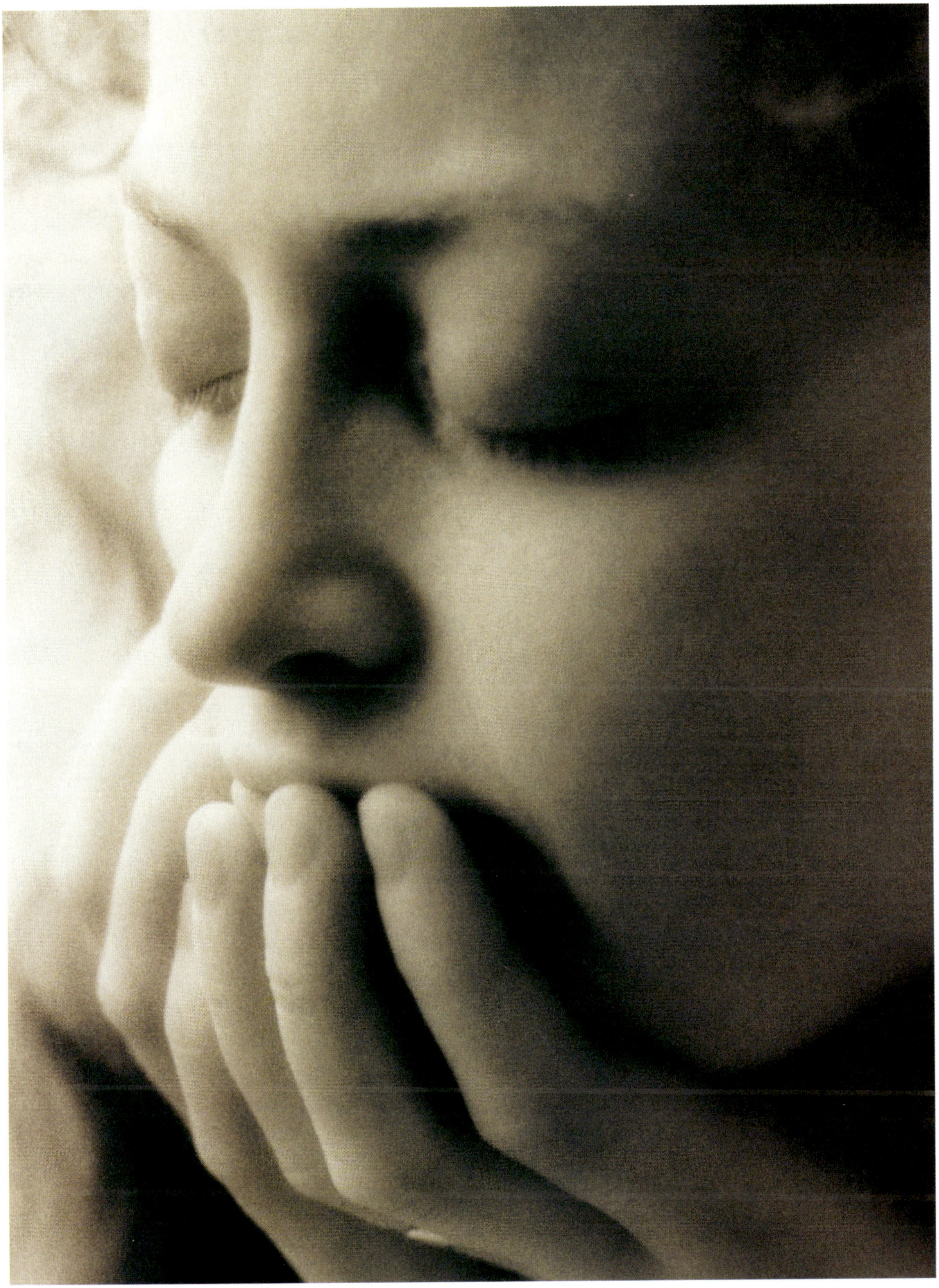

Reducing Meningitis Risk

Meningitis is a very serious infection causing inflammation of the *meninges* (the membranes covering the brain and the spinal cord) commonly affecting children (often as a complication of maternal TB, measles, mumps, whooping cough, or ear infection) although it can infect a person of any age. Meningitis may be *viral* or *bacterial*. The former does not necessarily need elaborate treatment. The latter constitutes a medical emergency.

The two most important causes of bacterial meningitis are *haemophilus influenza* and *meningococcal* infection. Meningococcal meningitis is globally epidemic and occurs in 'waves' of infection. In the wave 1996 to the present, 300,000 cases have been reported in sub-Saharan Africa. Even in non-peaking years there are around 1.2 million cases of bacterial meningitis a year worldwide and of these 500,000 are meningococcal and 50,000 of these cases die.

The 'Meningitis Belt'

The meningitis belt extends from Ethiopia to Senegal in sub-Saharan Africa with the condition occurring in the dry season of these countries. The highest proportion of those infected is found in young children and through to young adults.

Waves of infection reached their peak in Burkina Faso in 1984-5 with 15,000 and 1997 with just over 40,000; Niger in 1967 with 20,000 and 1996 with a little over 25,000; Sudan in 1979 with just under 30,000 and in 1989 with just over 30,000; Ethiopia in 1982 with a little under 40,000 and 1990 with just under 50,000. These waves often occur as a result of a smaller localized and uncontrolled outbreak and will last at high rates for a couple of years. The organism responsible for the meningococcal meningitis *(Neisseria meningitidis)* has a variety of strains so there may be waning immunity against a particular strain, thus putting populations at risk.

Signs and Symptoms

The incubation period for meningitis is from two to ten days but averaging three to four days. Signs and symptoms include the following:

- flu-like in viral meningitis;
- fever;
- stiff neck. Child looks very sick and lies with head and neck bent back;
- severe headache;
- back too stiff to put head between the knees;
- In babies under 1 year the *fontanel* (soft spot on top of head) bulges upward;
- child, very sleepy; adults, lethargic, delirious;
- nausea and vomiting common;
- maybe fits or strange movements;
- condition worsens until unconscious;
- rash of tiny red spots which turn into purple marks;

In babies under 1 year the *fontanel* (soft spot on top of head) bulges upward.

The infection is spread by direct contact and inhaling the droplets of sneezing and coughing by infected persons. Conditions associated with deprivation also

Reducing Meningitis Risk 75

favour the spread of infection as do prolonged drought and dust storms. Even with early and adequate therapeutic intervention there may be a 5 – 10 per cent fatality rate. In the absence of treatment this may exceed 50 per cent. Of the people with meningococcal meningitis who recover from the infection, 15 –20 per cent may have deafness, mental retardation, or other neurological conditions due to the infection.

Prevention and Treatment

- BCG vaccination at birth will help prevent tubercular meningitis;
- One type of bacterial meningitis can be prevented by Hib vaccination of those at risk, however, antibiotics give effective protection to most people having contact with persons who already have meningitis;
- On the whole, vaccines have not been very successful due to the variety of strains involved and the limited duration of the effect of the vaccine, nor can they halt the progress of an epidemic unless they are targeted at a known serogroup.

GET IMMEDIATE MEDICAL HELP

- Try the glass 'pressure' test if a rash is present by pressing the bottom of the glass against the spots anywhere on the skin and viewing the result through the glass (a meningitis rash will not fade on pressure);

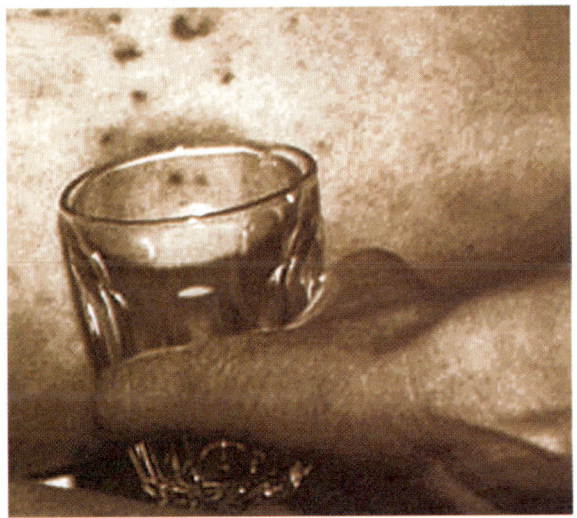

- Use wet cloths or fans to lower any fever;
- A lumbar puncture to test the cerebrospinal fluid is used to confirm the diagnosis;
- Antibiotic drugs will be prescribed, depending on the type of meningitis, or other therapeutic measures as necessary.

Long term implications for the control of a variety of medical conditions lie in changing, as far as possible, the social factors that favour the spread of disease.

A rash of tiny red spots which turn into purple marks

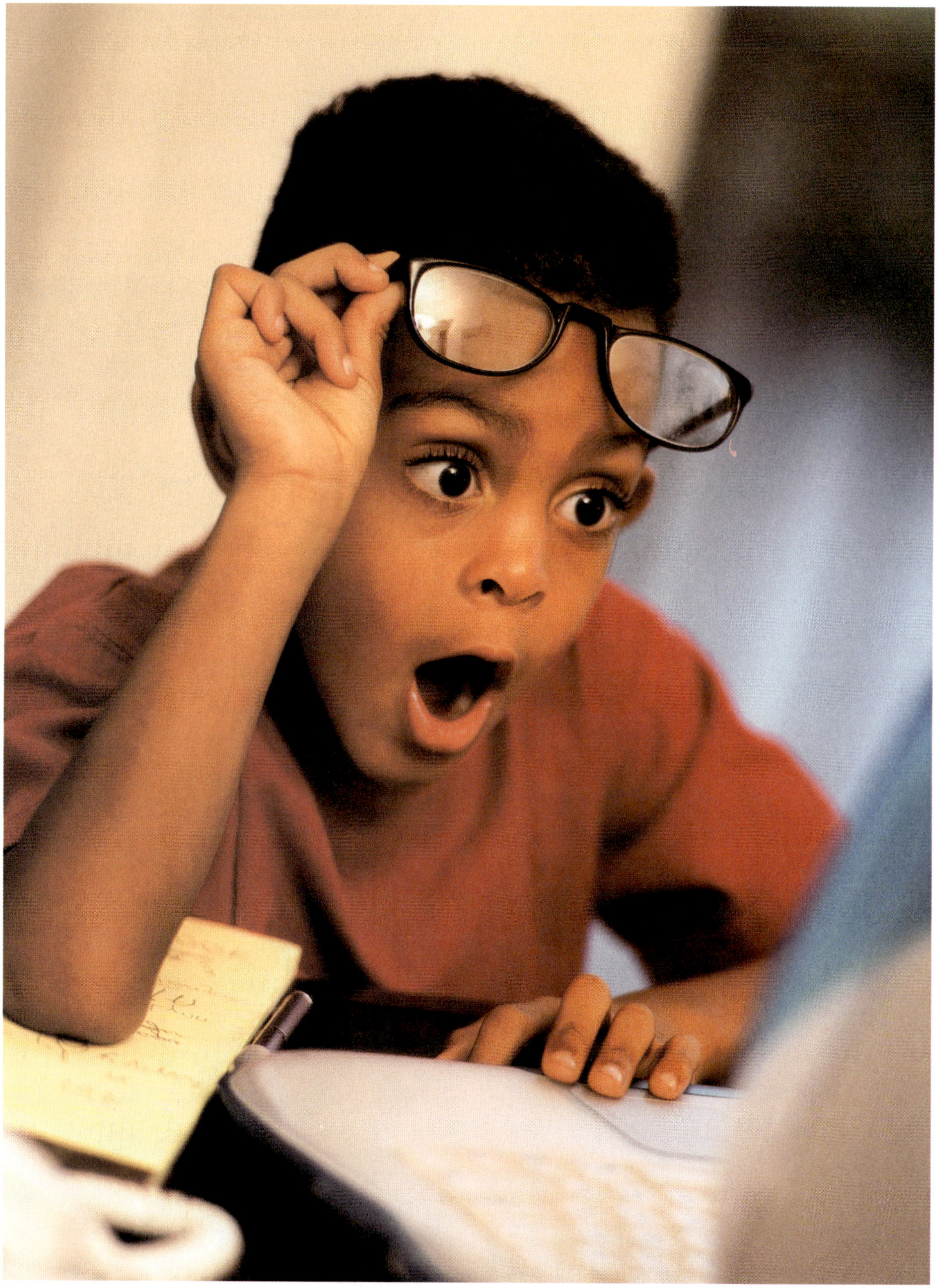

How to Help Your Eyes

It is only when something goes wrong with them that we value our eyes. These delicate structures need to be well looked after and medical help obtained if there are any problems. Personal hygiene and diet help to keep our eyes in excellent condition but we cannot avoid all the risks.

Get help immediately from a nurse, doctor, or clinic, if any of the following occur:

- Anything going into the eye and causing damage;
- Pain or pressure in the eye;
- Infection or inflammation that has not got better within a week since the start;
- Blurring or failing of vision in one or both eyes;
- Greyish spots on the cornea with reddening of the area around it;
- Difference in the size of the pupils, especially if there is any eye or head pain.

If you are not sure what is causing the problem or if the eye is injured keep the eye (or eyes) clean and covered with a patch or soft bandage and get help.

Do not try to remove anything that is embedded in the eye.

Small grit or dirt which has blown into the eye can be removed by flooding the eye with clean water, or by using the corner of a moist clean cloth.

It is unwise to use common remedies or ointments in the eye unless prescribed for the particular condition.

Beautiful eyes...

'It is only when something goes wrong with them that we value our eyes. These delicate structures need to be well looked after...'

The Normal Eye

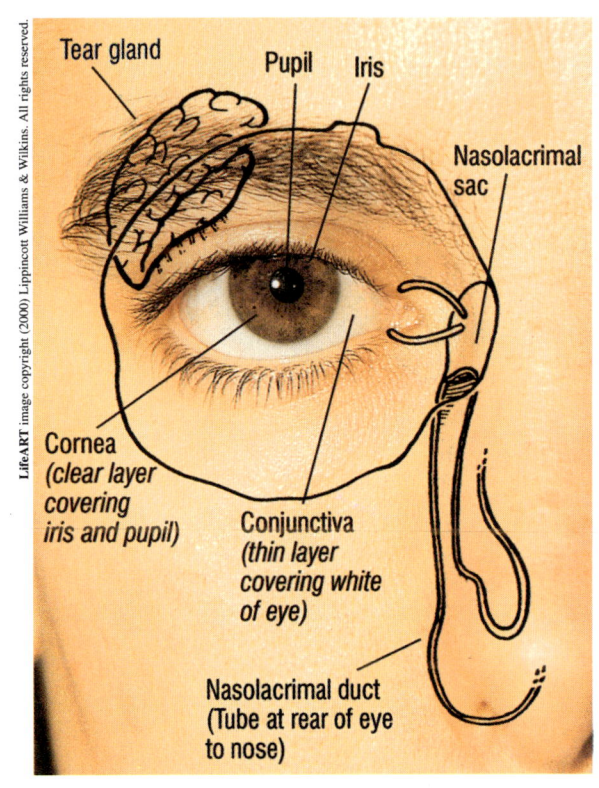

Tear gland
Pupil
Iris
Nasolacrimal sac
Cornea (clear layer covering iris and pupil)
Conjunctiva (thin layer covering white of eye)
Nasolacrimal duct (Tube at rear of eye to nose)

Pupil Irregularity

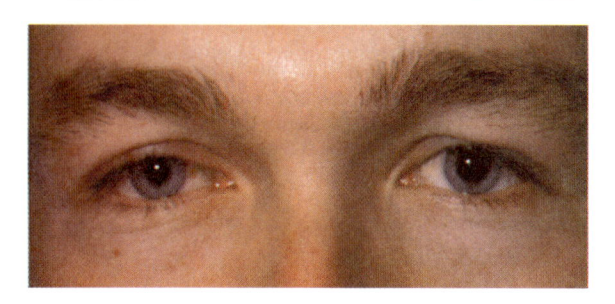

Difference in the size of the pupils may be due to:

- brain damage;
- glaucoma;
- injury;
- iritis;
- stroke.

Some irregularity of pupil size is normal in a few people.

Bleeding Behind the Cornea

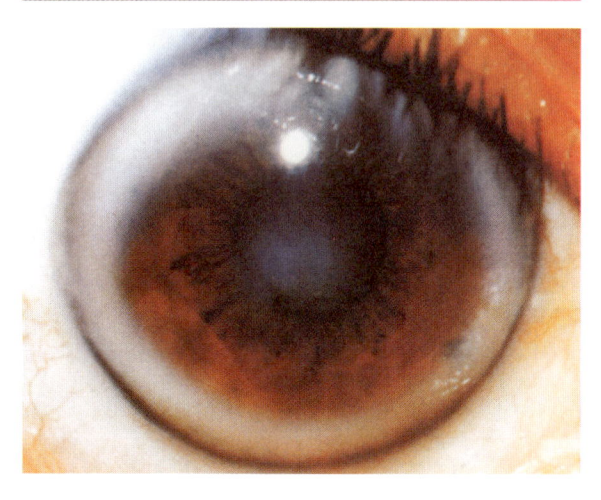

- Usually resulting from direct injury with a blunt object.

Treatment

- Eye patch;
- Rest;
- Get professional help.

Bleeding in the White of the Eye

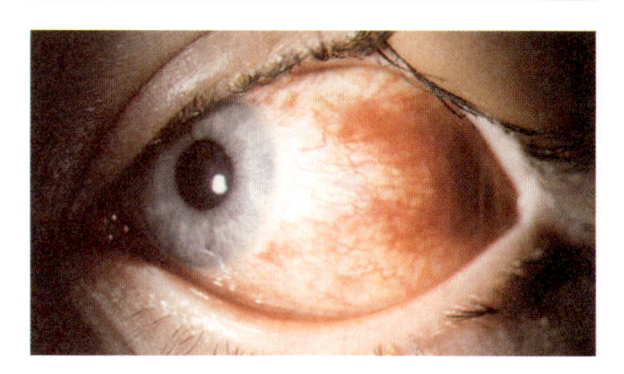

- Painless;
- Heavy lifting or hard coughing causing blood vessel to burst.

Treatment
- Usually clears without treatment.

Cataract

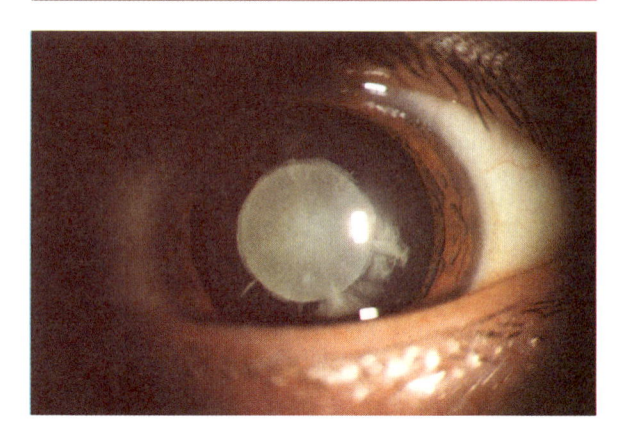

- Lens becomes cloudy grey or white;
- Occurs in older persons as a result of hardening and shrinking of the lens of the eye;
- Can also be the result of injury or irradiation by ultraviolet or infra-red light.

Treatment
- Surgery at the appropriate time.

Corneal Ulcer

- Resulting from scrape, or infection;
- May be less shiny than surrounding tissue.

How to Help Your Eyes 79

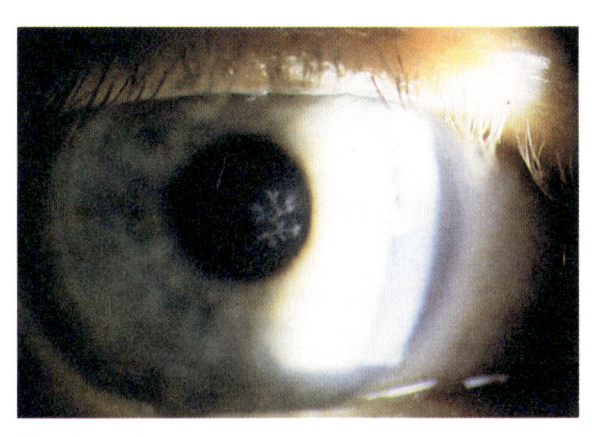

Treatment
+ Antibiotic eye ointment and other antibiotics;
+ Eye patch.

Corneal Scar

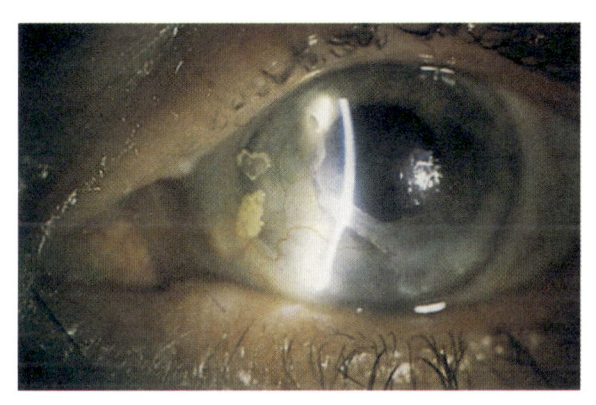

+ Painless white patch on the cornea as a result of burn, ulcer, or other injury.

Treatment
+ If justified a corneal transplant may be carried out by an eye surgeon.

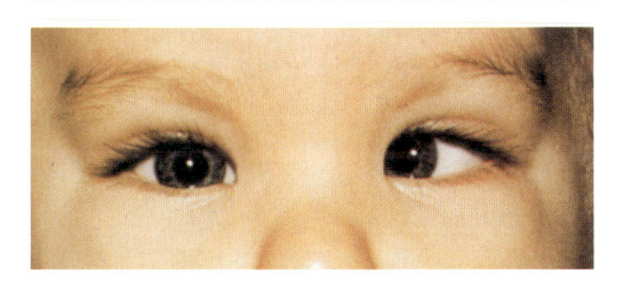

Cross Eyes

+ Eye that turns in or out or wanders.

Treatment
+ 6 months old: keep good eye covered until poor eye stays straight;
+ Above 6 months seek professional advice;
+ Surgical correction.

Glaucoma

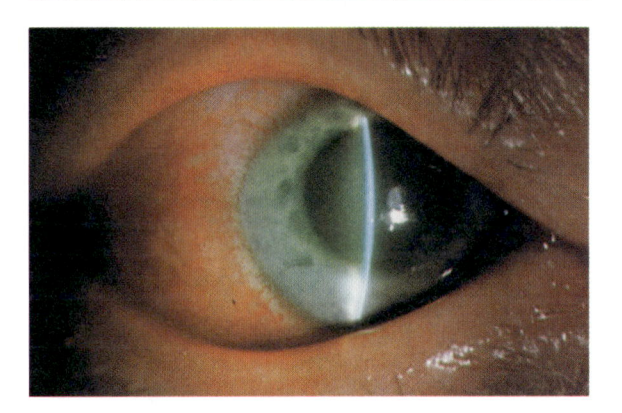

+ Pressure within the eye;
+ Usually begins after age 40, affecting one per cent of people above that age;
+ Common cause of blindness;
+ represents about 15-20 per cent of ophthalmologic work.

Acute glaucoma:
+ Severe eye pain;
+ Headache;
+ Reddening of eye;
+ Blurring of vision;
+ Eyeball hard to the touch;
+ Enlarged pupil.

Treatment
+ Immediate medical help.

Chronic glaucoma:
+ Slow build-up of pressure in the eye;
+ Usually painless;
+ Slow loss of vision starting from the side.

Treatment

- Immediate medical help;
- Vision test, particularly side vision;
- Eyedrops to prevent blindness;
- Eye pressure tests and appropriate medication to reduce raised pressure;
- Where surgical intervention is required Afro-Caribbeans have a higher surgical failure rate.

General observations

- Annual eye tests, especially if over 40 years old and where relatives have glaucoma. Their pressures should also be checked annually;
- Early recognition of the signs and symptoms of glaucoma hold out best hope of avoiding blindness.

Infected Eyes

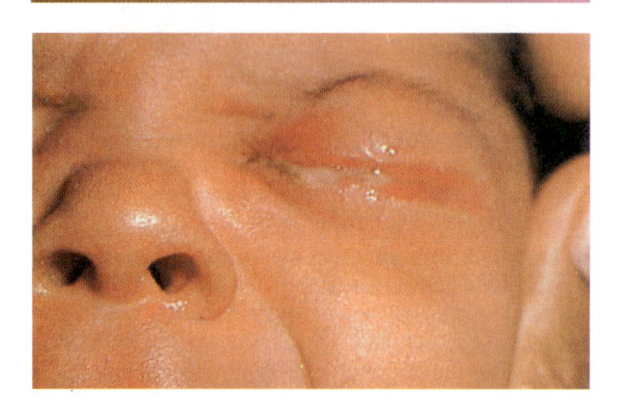

In newborn babies *(Neonatal Conjunctivitis)*

- Usually as a result of contact with disease in the mother;
- Where the baby's eye is red, swollen and exuding pus the cause is probably gonorrhoea.

Treatment

- Immediate medical help;
- Both parents treated for gonorrhoea.

Infection of the Tear Sac

- Pain, swelling and redness beneath the eye and affecting the nose;
- Watering of the affected eye;
- Small amounts of pus in the corner of the eye if gentle pressure applied to affected area.

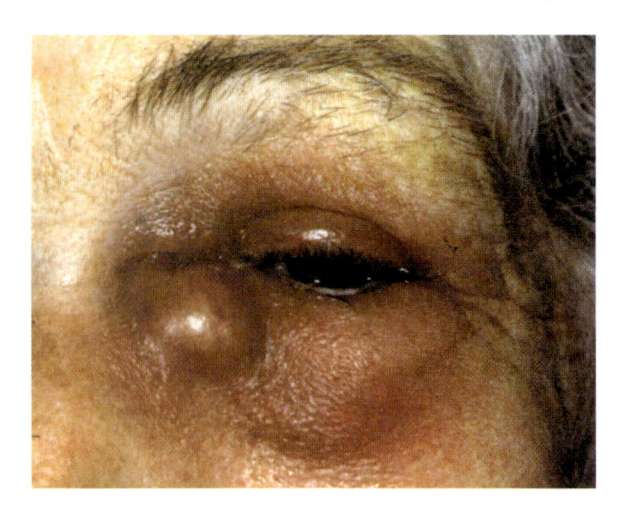

Treatment

- Hot compresses;
- Get medical help as antibiotic eye drops and other antibiotics will be required.

Iritis

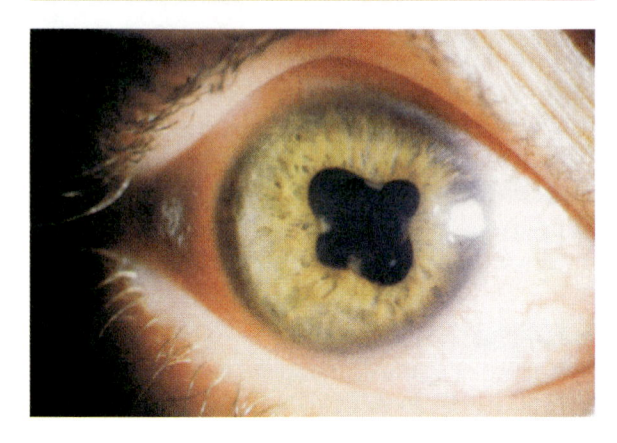

- Inflammation of the iris;
- Blurring of vision and eye watering, reaction to bright light;
- Sudden or gradual pain becoming severe;
- Redness around iris;
- Pupils small and often irregularly shaped.

Treatment

- Immediate medical help.

How to Help Your Eyes 81

Night Blindness and Xerosis

- Vitamin A deficiency, common in children aged 2-5 years;
- Difficulty with seeing during hours of darkness;
- Eyes develop dry, wrinkly patches (xerosis) and lose their shine;
- Little grey bubbles (Bitot's spots) start to form on eyes;
- If untreated in the early stage, the cornea dries and dulls and pitting of the cornea may develop;
- The cornea quickly softens, bulges and even bursts;
- These painless occurrences may result in blindness from infection, scarring, or damage;
- Xerosis often occurs as a result of childhood sicknesses causing vitamin A deficiency.

Treatment
- Eat foods rich in vitamin A (these include fruits and vegetables). Where the diet lacks these items vitamin supplements are prescribed;
- Night blindness may be prevented by breast feeding a baby up to age 2 where possible;
- Children with illnesses likely to cause vitamin deficiency or if underweight should have their eyes checked for any of the above signs or symptoms of night blindness, and be given appropriate treatment.

'Pink Eye' Conjunctivitis

- Inflammation of the conjunctiva of one or both eyes;
- Redness of outer eye, with burning sensation and varying amounts of pus;
- Eyelids may stick together.

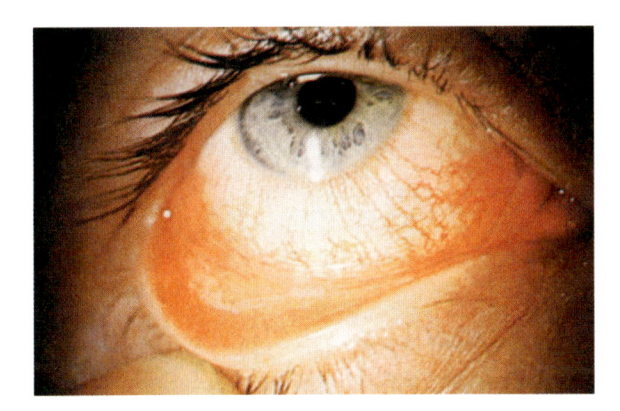

Treatment
- Good eye cleanliness;
- Antibiotics;
- Hygiene measures to avoid passing on infection.

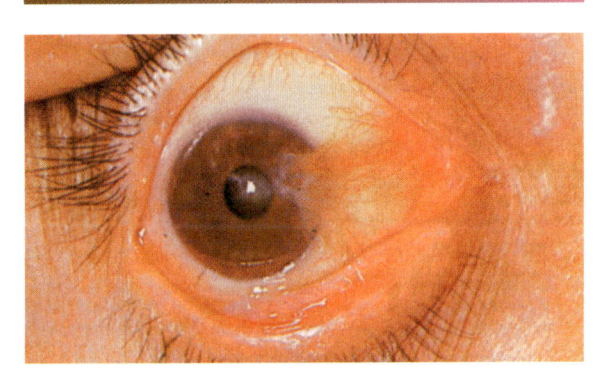

Pterygium

- A slow-growing fleshy thickening on the eye surface developing from the edge to the cornea;
- May be caused by dust, sunlight or wind.

Treatment
- Use of dark glasses to slow growth;
- Surgical removal before the pupil is affected.

Pus behind the Cornea

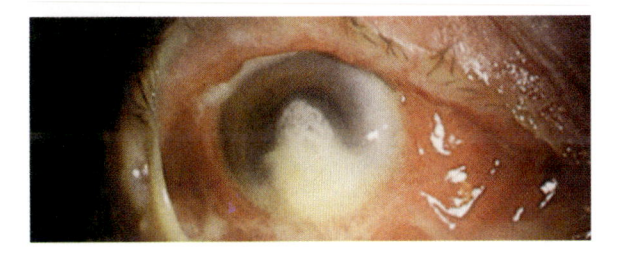

- Caused by severe inflammation often accompanying corneal ulcers.

Treatment
- Get immediate medical help;
- Antibiotic treatment.

Stye

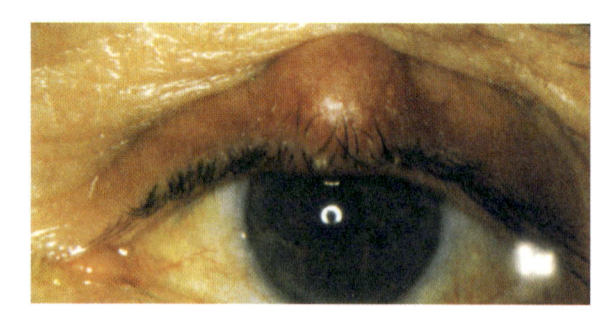

- Inflammation of the tear duct causing painful swelling around the edge of the eyelid.

Treatment
- Warm salt water compress;
- Antibiotics.

Long or Short Sight

- Headaches and eye pain may be caused by difficulty in seeing clearly.

Treatment
- Eyesight tests or other tests to establish cause of difficulties;
- Glasses prescribed if necessary.

Trachoma

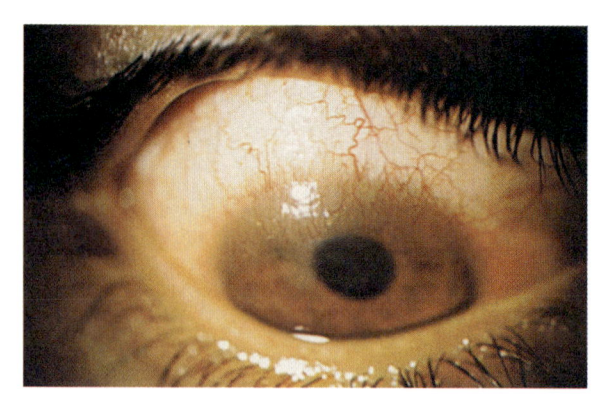

- Chronic form of conjunctivitis caused by a microorganism and lasting many years, sometimes bringing blindness;
- Spread by touch, flies, and poor hygiene;
- Red watery eyes;
- Pinkish grey follicles form inside the upper eyelids;
- White of the eye mildly inflamed;
- Upper edge of cornea looks greyish because of minute new blood vessels *(pannus)*;
- The follicles and *pannus* are a certain diagnosis of trachoma;
- When the follicles begin to disappear, after some years, white scars remain.

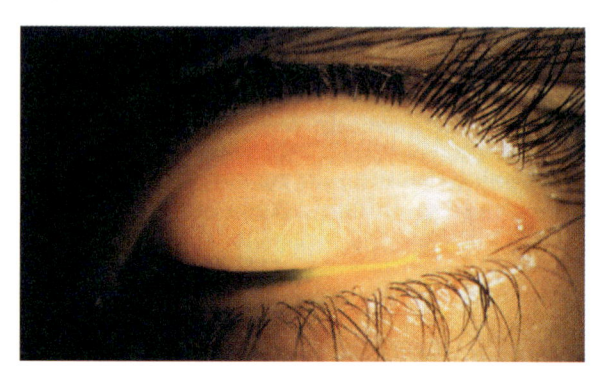

- The eyelids are thickened by the scars and stop the eyes from opening and closing all the way;
- Blindness may be caused by the lids being pulled down and scratching the eye, resulting in corneal damage.

Treatment
- Get immediate medical help;
- Antibiotics administered topically and systemically;
- Continued eye and general cleanliness.

Double Vision

+ Double vision experienced from time to time could be a sign of exhaustion, or weakness caused by a poor diet;
+ Sudden double vision is a sign of a chronic, or progressively serious, problem;
+ Spots or small moving objects in the field of vision.

Treatment
+ Rest and regular nourishing meals;
+ Get immediate medical help.

River Blindness

+ Extremely minute hump-backed flies known as *simulids* inject worms *onchocerca volvulus* as they go from person to person;
+ The flies breed and swarm near fast-moving streams. Their bite causes a reaction which may result in blindness if in the vicinity of the eyes.

Treatment
+ Diethylcarbamizine drug therapy,
+ Anti-insect measures.

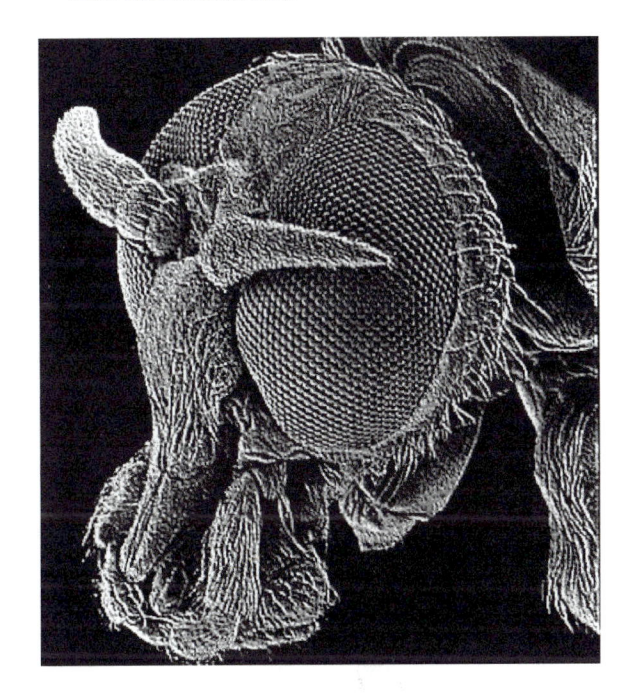

How to Help Your Eyes 83

84   How to Stay Healthy

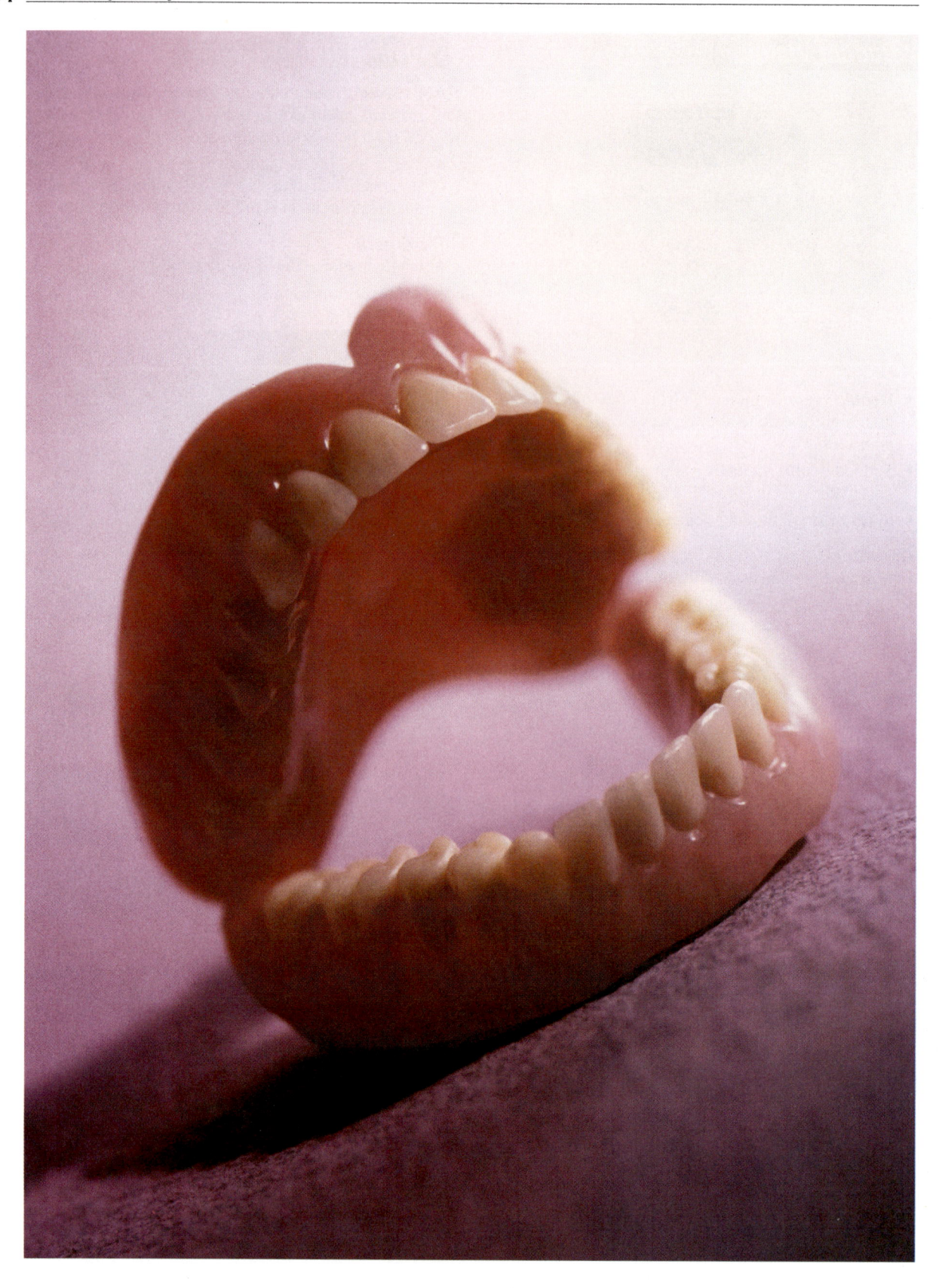

How to Help Your Teeth and Mouth

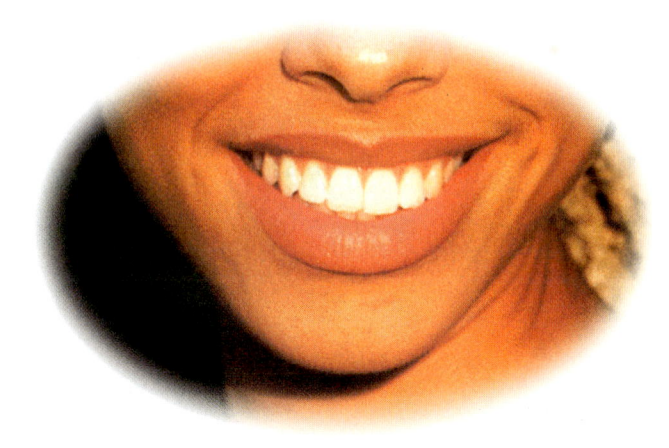

Prevention and Treatment

- Avoid sweets, cakes, sugars, cola drinks and biscuits;
- Rinse mouth with warm salt water;
- Brush teeth after meals:
  – brush the lower teeth up and the top teeth down,
  – brush the front and back of the teeth;
- Have regular dental checks;
- Have fillings and polishing as required;
- Where possible have regular, well-nourishing meals.

- Good teeth are needed to chew food well.
- There are usually two sets of teeth:

  – **Baby teeth**   **20 teeth**
    appearing 5-8 months
                    8-10 months
                    1-3 years

  – **Permanent teeth**   **32 teeth**
                              molars
    (back teeth) 5-6 years
          wisdom   16+ years

- Good tooth care prevents teeth cavities and sore gums.
- Infections in the mouth can spread to other parts of the body.

- *Pyorrhea*

A disease of the gums with infection and loose teeth due to poor hygiene and inadequate nutrition.

- *Halitosis*

Bad breath caused by rotten teeth cavities filling with food and poor mouth hygiene.

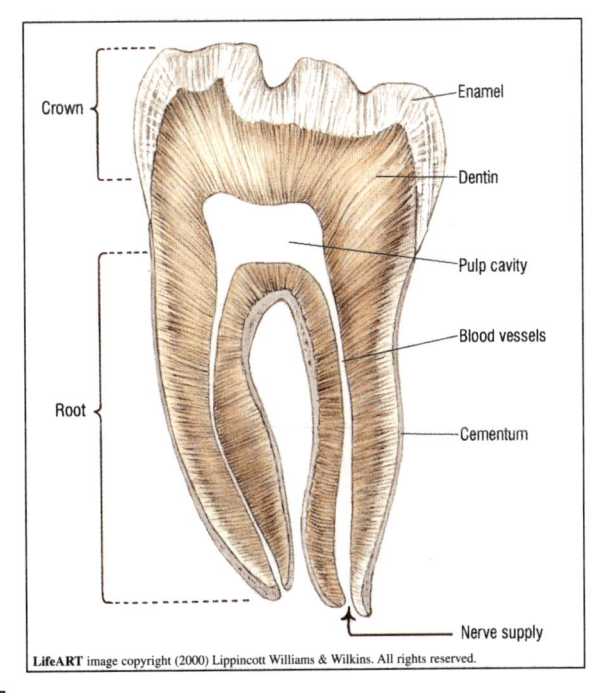

Tooth diagram labels: Crown, Enamel, Dentin, Pulp cavity, Blood vessels, Root, Cementum, Nerve supply

LifeART image copyright (2000) Lippincott Williams & Wilkins. All rights reserved.

86 How to Stay Healthy

How to Help Your Ears

Your ears are important not only for your hearing – which is important enough – but also for your sense of balance. Each ear consists of three main parts:

- *outer* and *middle* ear, mostly concerned with the collection and transmission of sound, and
- the *inner* ear which contains the apparatus which helps the body to maintain its balance.

Anything which interferes with hearing or balance should be reported to your health-care provider.

The Normal Ear

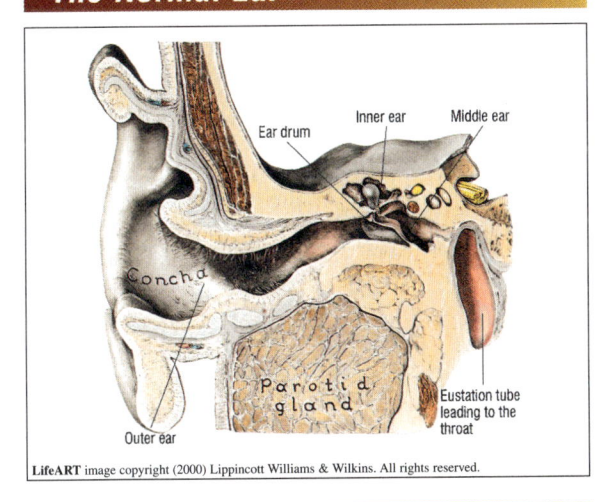

Disorders of the Ear

Earache is the most common disorder of the ear, signalling a localized problem of any of the three parts of the ear or in any of the adjacent structures such as the throat or the teeth.

When the ear is examined, the nose and throat will also be examined for possible contributing causes.

Causes of earache include the following:

- *Otitis externa*
    inflammation or infection in the external ear;
    such as an abscess or boil;
    there may be irritation in the ear canal which produces a thin watery or thicker pus-filled discharge (*otorrhea*);
    hearing loss might occur in severe cases.

- *Otitis media*
    infection of the middle ear;
    particularly common in young children;
    person likely to have a raised temperature;
    the pain may be stabbing and severe;
    likely to be hearing loss;
    infection may cause perforation of the eardrum and subsequent discharge of pus from the middle ear;
    condition may be linked to dental problems or tonsilitis;
    if untreated the infection may spread to the bone behind the middle ear (*mastoiditis*).

The underlying cause of these conditions will be treated and antibiotics prescribed. It may be necessary to perforate the eardrum surgically to release the pus in the middle ear, and in both conditions pus may be drained off (*myringotomy*).

- Other disorders of the ear – particularly affecting the inner ear – include: *labyrinthitis* in which the balance mechanism is affected, with resultant giddiness (*vertigo*) and hearing loss; and *Meniérè's disease* in which the small oscillating bones become fixed, also affecting balance and hearing.

- *Obstructions* of the ear are also common, especially when children insert small objects into the ear canal, but insects and the build-up of wax are commoner causes. Firmly fixed objects may need medical attention to remedy. Insects can be floated out of the ear by tilting the head and dropping small amounts of clean water or olive oil into the canal. The head can then be tilted in the opposite direction and the insect freed. If wax is a problem let your health-care provider decide whether drops or syringing (or both) is appropriate.

Keeping the ears clean and drying them thoroughly after swimming and/or showering will help to keep these organs in fine form and able to do their work.

88 How to Stay Healthy

Reducing Risk Using Home Treatments

Home Treatment

There are many common conditions occurring at home which can be relieved by using fairly simple measures. Water and a few household items may be all that is required to stop a minor medical incident becoming a major crisis. Such conditions, along with their treatments, include:

- Burns
  - immersion in cold water.
- Cough
  - steam inhalation, heating compress, hot foot bath. Gargling with warm salty water may take away some of the irritation of a sore throat.
- Fever
  - *with flush* – tepid sponging.
  - *with pallor* (pale skin) – hot sponging.
- General weakness and fatigue
  - hot and cold spray or warm bath.
- Headache
  - cold compress to head, hot foot bath.
- Insomnia
  - tepid bath or sheet pack.
- Sprain
  - alternate application of heat and cold, bath, compress, ice-pack.

Action and Reaction

These simple treatments work because the application of cold and heat changes the blood supply in the area treated. Heat increases the supply by enlarging the blood vessels and, conversely, cold constricts the blood vessels, so restricting the blood supply.

There are three temperatures to keep in mind while using the following remedies:

- The boiling point of water is   212°F or 100°C
- Human body temperature is   98°F or 37°C
- The freezing point of water is   32°F or 0°C

Specific Applications

- *Burns:*
  Completely immerse the burnt or scalded area in cold water. Do not use iced water. Keep the burnt area immersed in the water for about 10 minutes.
- *Cough:*
  If the nose, throat or chest is congested fill a bowl with boiling water, place a towel over the affected person's head to make a tent over the steam, then get them to breathe in and out deeply. Wait to start the treatment if the steam from the water is too hot.
- *Fever:*
  Where the individual is flushed the body can be sponged with tepid (cool) water; or wrap the person in a cool wet sheet; and/or use a well positioned electric fan. If the person is pallid (skin pale) use hot (not boiling) water and sponge and cover with extra blankets. Send for medical help.
- *General weakness or fatigue:*
  A body-temperature bath followed by restful sleep will help to restore a feeling of wellbeing.
- *Headache:*
  Cold compresses applied to the forehead and the area above and in front of the ears will help to relieve the tension-type headache; also soaking the feet in hot water, so causing a shift in blood flow, may ease a headache. Ensure, also, a good daily fluid intake to prevent headaches associated with dehydration.
- *Insomnia:*
  A body-temperature bath helps to promote sleep. Hot and cold showers may be necessary if the sleeplessness is a continuing problem.
- *Sprains:*
  If the sprains are in the extremities then hot and cold showers will reduce swelling. The water

should be as hot as is bearable, without inflicting damage; and as cold as possible. Start with the cold water first then plunge and cover the affected part in the hot water. Alternate between the two at least 6-8 times. Cold compresses can be applied to other areas of sprain. A normal hot-water bath may bring relief to some sprains, the application of ice-packs may help others. (Packets of frozen vegetables can be used in place of more elaborate ice-packs.)

Common sense will indicate whether or not medical help is needed. Send someone for help while applying these simple but effective treatments.

Feeling Good All Over!

You do not have to wait until you are sick to enjoy the benefits of water. Water can also be used as a general tonic to the system. Drinking 6-8 glasses of water daily aids the digestive and chemical processes in the body. More might be required where the environment causes loss of body fluid through sweating.

An ordinary face cloth or flannel mitten can be used to tone the blood circulation and help you to keep alert and feeling good all over. Take the cloth or mitten and soak it in cold water then rub the arm or leg vigorously until you get a glowing feeling. Increase the area rubbed each day until the whole body is involved. Keep the flannel wet but not running with cold water. This technique is often referred to as cold mitten friction. To save time a towel could be used to apply friction to the trunk and back of the body (occasionally dipping the towel in a bowl of cold water and wringing out any excess water before use). If used regularly the blood circulation in the body will be good and the body's immune system strengthened. This will lead to resistance against some of the common infections that come round from year to year, and will give all-round good health.

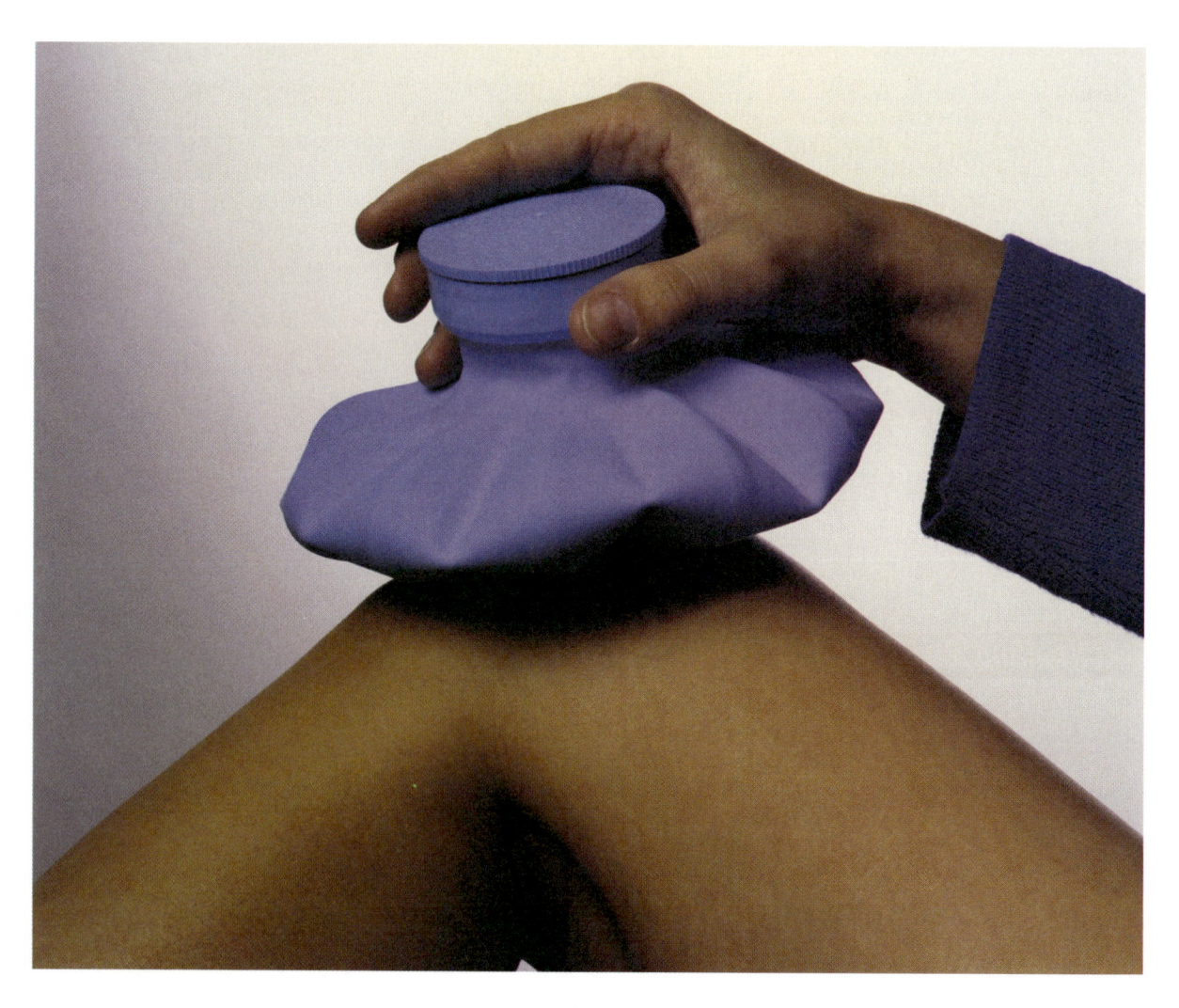

Reducing Risk Using Home Treatments

Reducing the Risk of Sexually-Transmitted Disease

It is a source of great concern to health-care providers that, in spite of increasing knowledge in the area of sex education, sexually-transmitted diseases (STDs) are on the increase worldwide. There are 333 million cases of curable STDs reported annually. Too many people are either ignorant of the risks they run or are deliberately courting the risk as an added 'excitement' in their personal lifestyle. Men and women in the age range 20-24 are the most exposed to risk.

Sexually-Transmitted Diseases

Excluding, for the moment, AIDS *(Acquired Immune Deficiency Syndrome)*, the four most common of the STDs are (with their worldwide incidence): *Syphilis* (12 million); *Gonorrhea* (62 million); *Chlamydia* (89 million); and *Trichomoniasis* (170 million).

These conditions can be treated fairly easily with antibiotics and/or antibacterials. Untreated, a wide range of complications can develop. Successful treatment does not confer immunity so the individual is susceptible to reinfection.

HIV/AIDS

Of the STDs, the United Nations and the World Health Organization report that AIDS has surpassed tuberculosis to become the world's biggest fatal disease (sadly, because of their vulnerable condition, and shared environmental circumstances, many AIDS patients die of TB). Not all AIDS infection is through sexual contact but in the majority of cases it is.

Sixty-three per cent of the world's HIV infection, affecting some 35 million people, is to be found in sub-Saharan Africa, which has had 10.25 million deaths from the infection to date. East African women and children are six times as likely to be infected as their male contemporaries. This is because they are more likely to have sex before the age of 15 and often marry older men as compared with other African states.

HIV stands for *Human Immunodeficiency Virus*, an organism first isolated in the early 1980s. The virus attacks the immune system at a faster rate than the production of antibodies, so making the body's defence system useless. Some people carry the virus without producing any symptoms, in others a cluster of symptoms (or syndrome) is observed. The time span for the development of *AIDS* with the following symptoms is varied:

- extensive tiredness with no obvious cause and lasting for several weeks;

- fever and night sweats also perhaps lasting for a number of weeks;

- persistent diarrhoea with no obvious cause;

- persistent dry cough and shortness of breath;

- skin disease characterized by hard pink/purple/dark blotches appearing on the eyelids and/or mouth and closely resembling blood blisters or bruises;

- swollen glands, usually in the neck and armpits;

- unexpected weight loss (in excess of 10 lb/4.5kg over a two-month period).

People with these symptoms go on to develop serious diseases centred on the lungs, digestive and central nervous system. In particular *Kaposi's sarcoma* (a rare skin cancer), and *pneumocystis carinii* pneumonia. About one third of HIV carriers will go on to develop these life-threatening conditions. As there is no test for AIDS, the diagnosis will rest on the observation of the above symptoms and the presence of antibodies in the blood of the infected individual.

Preventing Infection

Sexual abstinence in general and limiting sex to one faithful partner in the enriching experience of marriage is still the best means of prevention. Prevention of the spread of STDs is a lifestyle matter in which a number of factors will play a motivating role. In an ideal world this would be enough to reduce the risk to a minimum.

Many people are not concerned about the risk, or hold to a different set of values. These individuals need to be encouraged to practise safer sex for everyone's benefit by:

✦ limiting their partners – the more partners, the greater the risk;

✦ thinking carefully before sex – obvious signs of disease or infection might be present;

✦ using a sheath (condom) or diaphragm, though while these may reduce risk they do not confer absolute protection;

✦ practising good hygiene – washing the genital area with soap and water after intercourse may help to reduce risk of *some* infections;

✦ telling their partner – it is criminal to have an infection and not to pass on that information to the other partner(s) involved.

Everyone's Responsibility

If STDs are to be eliminated from society then everybody has a responsibility to ensure that it happens:

✦ Parents
    must learn everything they can about STDs, however distasteful this might be; they need to communicate values and information;

✦ School and local service agencies should
    seek to inform students;
    establish clinics and treatment centres liaising with medical facilities.

✦ Young People should
    learn about sex in its proper context and recognize the risks from casual and/or unprotected sex and know what remedial steps can be taken;
    avoid infection by not being sexually promiscuous.

✦ Faith Communities need to
    nurture their young people and encourage them to discuss issues of a sexual nature in a non-threatening way;
    impart values by example;
    be accepting and caring in the face of human weakness.

✦ Health-care Professionals need to
    engage in vigorous health promotion and resource all of the above in their learning experience;
    deal with STDs openly;
    promptly report STDs to the follow-up agencies.

Prompt reporting of STDs will result in an early diagnosis and timely treatment generally but particularly in the case of HIV/AIDS. Sexual partners should also be checked, ensuring, once again, early treatment where necessary and peace of mind. Do not discontinue treatment before completing the prescribed regime and do not miss follow-up appointments.

One reason STDs are so difficult to stamp out is that the chain of sexual contacts among those having these diseases is complicated. One man or woman may infect a large number of other men or women, who pass the infection on to still other men and women, in a spiralling web of heterosexual and homosexual contacts.

Adapted from a *These Times* supplement 1974.

Postscript

There are many reasons for wanting to be healthy and staying healthy. The more of these you can include in your motivation the better your health will be.

Staying healthy requires planning and sustained effort, especially in the formation of good health habits. In an age of dwindling health resources, anything that we can do to help ourselves will be worth the effort. Being healthy should also be fun, and while it appears to be a long list of does and don'ts, with practice these become second nature. Good habits are caught rather than taught, so remember to take it easy on the people around you.

A good sense of humour is also required. It is health-bestowing in its own right, and also helps to put more serious things into a different perspective.

If, along with all the above, you can cultivate a deep, abiding faith, you will have the best of both worlds! Share what you find both individually and through your faith community.

Do not lose sight of the fact that you are unique – *someone* special deserves special care.